D1253006

"This book reminds us of what is most important and not to be taken for granted — and how to align our lives with that vital awakening to the beauty and possibility that is always present amidst the darkness and the fear."

— **JON KABAT-ZINN,** founder of MBSR (mindfulness-based stress reduction) and author of *Full Catastrophe Living* and *Mindfulness for All*

"With Kristi Nelson's guidance we are prepared to hold our lives tenderly, be kind, and love each other fully."

— **MARIA SIROIS,** Psy.D., author of *A Short Course in Happiness After Loss*

"If Kristi Nelson's five guiding principles were pinned to every bathroom mirror, not only would we wake up grateful, but we would most certainly wake up to a different world."

— **NIPUN MEHTA,** founder, ServiceSpace

"Kristi Nelson has written a soul-revealing and stirring companion for life's peaks and valleys. I'm grateful for her wisdom and this book."

— **RACHEL BAGBY,** founder, Singing Farm Sanctuary

"Cancer taught Kristi Nelson to accept the uncertainty and impermanence of life, and through that she discovered gratefulness as a path to healing and wholeness. Now she offers it to us, and it is a blessing to receive."

— **MIRABAI BUSH,** Senior Fellow, The Center for Contemplative Mind in Society and coauthor with Ram Dass of *Walking Each Other Home*

Wake Up GRATEFUL

The Transformative Practice of Taking Nothing for Granted

KRISTI NELSON

A Network for Grateful Living

FOREWORD BY BROTHER DAVID STEINDL-RAST

Storey Publishing

The mission of Storey Publishing is to serve our customers by
publishing practical information that encourages
personal independence in harmony with the environment.

EDITED BY Deborah Balmuth, Liz Bevilacqua, and Nina Shield

ART DIRECTION AND BOOK DESIGN BY Alethea Morrison

TEXT PRODUCTION BY Erin Dawson

WATERCOLORS BY © Nomoco

The following poems were reprinted with permission
Page 74: "We Look with Uncertainty" by Anne Hillman, *The Dancing Animal Woman: A Celebration of Life*, 1994, 3rd Printing, 2007. Bramble Books. www.annehillman.net.
Page 90: Excerpted from "Hymn, with Birds and Cats" by Francine Marie Tolf

Page 104: "Laughter" by Dale Biron, *Why We Do Our Daily Practices* © 2014, Pack Mule Press
Page 118: "Rethinking Regret" by Elaine Sexton
Page 135: "Darn Lucky" by Rosemerry Wahtola Trommer, originally published on A Network for Grateful Living's website, https://gratefulness.org
Page 152: "The Unbroken" by Rashani Réa. Written in 1991 following the fifth death in her family. www.rashani.com.
Page 166: "What I Want and What I Can Have" by Jeanie Greensfelder, from *I Got What I Came For* (Penciled In, 2017)
Page 196: "Benediction" by Bernadette Miller
Page 211–212: "Hokusai Says" by Roger Keyes

Text © 2020 by A Network for Grateful Living

Storey books are available at special discounts when purchased in bulk for premiums and sales promotions as well as for fund-raising or educational use. Special editions or book excerpts can also be created to specification. For details, please call 800-827-8673, or send an email to sales@storey.com.

Storey Publishing
210 MASS MoCA Way
North Adams, MA 01247
storey.com

Printed in the United States
by LSC Communications
10 9 8 7 6 5 4 3 2 1

Library of Congress Cataloging-in-Publication Data

Names: Nelson, Kristi, author.
Title: Wake up grateful : the transformative practice of taking nothing for granted/ Kristi Nelson, A Network for Grateful Living ; foreword by Brother David Steindl-Rast.
Description: North Adams : Storey Publishing, 2020.
Identifiers: LCCN 2020024841 (print) | LCCN 2020024842 (ebook) | ISBN 9781635862447 (hardcover) | ISBN 9781635862454 (ebook)
Subjects: LCSH: Gratitude. | Gratitude—Religious aspects. | Well-being.
Classification: LCC BF575.G68 N447 2020 (print) | LCC BF575.G68 (ebook) | DDC 179/.9—dc23
LC record available at https://lccn.loc.gov/2020024841
LC ebook record available at https://lccn.loc.gov/2020024842

DEDICATED TO

Brother David Steindl-Rast,
and all those committed to living gratefully

✳

My parents,
for giving me the gift of life
and then — each in their own way —
showing me how to love it
fiercely and with joy.

Contents

FOREWORD

The book you are holding in your hands has been written by a hero of mine. It is not the fruit of speculation, but has grown out of suffering and of heroic trust in life. Kristi Nelson discovered grateful living while struggling with stage IV cancer at age 33. She knows how it feels to face dying. But that very experience has taught her to speak with depth and weight when she is talking about living — grateful living. She knows the deep joy that springs from simply being alive and she can show you ways toward finding joy in your own life.

A miniformula for grateful living runs through this whole book. Kristi has unpacked and unfolded it, until it developed into this full-fledged guide to finding joy and well-being. The three-word formula is: *Stop. Look. Go.* Moment by moment, life is offering you gift after gift — exactly what you need to thrive. But unless you stop, you will rush right by that gift; unless you look, you will miss it; and only if you go and do something with it can you fully avail yourself of that gift.

Practice *Stop. Look. Go.* faithfully over and over, like practicing a dance step, and you will soon notice with surprise that you are getting more and more in step with life — that you had been out of step, without even noticing it. You practice dance steps in order to dance, and grateful living is a dance with life — life as it is, in all its ecstasies and also in its agonies. Grateful living is passionate interaction with the world in all its excitement, vulnerability, and risk.

Dare to take that risk and you will be drawn into an altogether unpredictable adventure. "I would wake up every morning and notice that I was still breathing," Kristi writes. "I would have to touch my face to make sure it was not a dream." Breathing with trust in life — that was enough. It was the risk she took. She realized, "I was still alive. And being alive was enough."

Coming alive means taking hold of whatever life is offering us, here and now. It is enough — and more than enough. And we may trust that it's exactly what we need — like it or not. Life knows best. Life deserves our trust. And there is no better exercise than *Stop. Look. Go.* to get us into shape for catching each moment's gift. Let's not allow it to slip through our fingers!

Catching the moment. Yes, that skill is what every page of this book wants to teach you: to catch the moment and to live in its fullness. Kristi Nelson is a coach you can trust. Right now, life is pitching her book your way.

Wake up!

BROTHER DAVID STEINDL-RAST, OSB
Azcuénaga, Argentina, January 2020

Wherever you are is the starting point.
—Kabir

INTRODUCTION

ALIVE AND GRATEFUL

Not dying changed everything. Not only did I not die, I actually got to live. And living offered me the chance to bring the most meaningful lessons I learned from facing death into my life and the lives of many others. What I have come to understand about taking nothing for granted has transformed my life. My hope is that it will transform yours too.

At 33 years old, I was diagnosed with stage IV Hodgkin's lymphoma that had metastasized to my spine. After going through 18 months of hospitalizations, surgeries, chemotherapy, and treatments, I asked my oncologist, "When will I be out of the woods?" He answered, "You will never be out of the woods." Having worked so hard to stay alive, I had not grasped the degree of uncertainty and struggle that would come with being a survivor. Understanding that my life would only ever be lived with the caveat of "for now" was sobering. I wondered so many things: How do I continue to live this way? What am I able to count on? How can I possibly plan for the future? How do I live while expecting to die?

The first few years of uncertainty and remission put the blessings of my life in sharp relief. I was in *super-soak* mode — every experience was saturated with new meaning, and I was absorbing it all fully. I did not know any other way to live the moments I had than to greet each one as gratefully as I could. Not sure how much more time was mine, I was awestruck by every moment, every person, and every thing. Being grateful the first few years was relatively easy and revelatory. I would wake up in a room bathed in light, hear birds singing, and notice I was still breathing. Sometimes I would have to touch my face to make sure it was not a dream. I could put both feet on the floor and walk freely to a kitchen where I could make a cup of tea. It was enough to make me start each day with tears of joy. Being alive was enough.

But over time, all those amazing reasons to feel grateful joined the ranks of the taken-for-granted. I got healthy and busy. I began chasing goals and the fulfillment they promised. I martyred myself to a job, complained about things like traffic, my weight, and colds. I ruthlessly compared myself to others, succumbed to retail therapy and debt, and suffered from stress. Each year that passed, I built up a kind of gratitude tolerance — what used to be enough got left in the dust in the pursuit of having more. Having cheated death, I began cheating life.

After some challenging years, dramatic wake-up calls, and my share of spiritual suffering, I came to realize that maintaining a grateful perspective is a true practice. Just as it takes commitment to keep a muscle strong, the same is true of perspective.

This capacity for grateful perspective is a muscle I needed to build and use, and it is still something I need to nurture and tend daily. I am the first to admit that I can lose perspective quite easily, so I work at it every day. But the practice of looking at the world through grateful eyes and with a grateful heart is an exquisite end in itself. I know it matters, and the results are worth everything.

Grateful living has become my way of life. It helps me focus on what is working and what is enough. It helps me notice all that is beautiful and breathtaking. Even in the most challenging times, from a grateful perspective I can see that there is an opportunity to learn, to deepen trust, to love, and to breathe. Fixing my awareness on what is available and possible in each moment — what is sufficient and sacred — I am less inclined to take life for granted. I am often filled to overflowing because of it, and this moves me to want to make a difference for others. Grateful living reconnects me with *a fidelity to life*. And this fidelity reminds me what a gift it is to be alive, and that it could always — and will someday — be otherwise.

Brother David

I first met Benedictine monk Brother David Steindl-Rast in 2003 when I was working with Lynne Twist at the Soul of Money Institute in San Francisco. One day, Lynne returned from a retreat at Upaya Zen Center in New Mexico with Brother David. I had no idea my life would be forever changed by this meeting.

Brother David was an intriguing paradox. In Birkenstock sandals with socks, a brown leather belt cinched at the waist of his black-and-white robes, shaved head gleaming above bushy eyebrows and sparkling eyes, he was both playful and sincere, magnetic and humble. I had lived in Germany when I was young, and I found Brother David's voice to be comforting, the familiarity of his accent lulling. I was not familiar with his teachings, but I knew that whatever his outlook on life, I was drawn to it.

Brother David and I joined Lynne and some friends for dinner and a performance of Cirque du Soleil, where we sat side by side gasping and holding our breath in unison as trapeze artists flew through the air making the seemingly impossible possible. The next morning before he departed, Brother David gave me his address and we exchanged a few letters over the following year. Many years later I learned that I was one of hundreds of people with whom he maintained a personal correspondence, some for many decades. His beautifully handwritten notes are a treasured keepsake in many a home and heart.

Over time, I learned that the roots of Brother David's teachings grew out of his teenage years in Vienna during World War II. He and his friends could not imagine a life beyond the war. When bombs fell, he would wait them out in a church basement, and when he emerged to the blue skies and silence of a new day, everything felt more vivid and alive. "The war made us live in the moment because the next moment a bomb may fall unknowingly," he said. "We lived every moment joyfully, not knowing if it would be our last. In the midst of this constant death, we were really joyful. When the war was over, there was a decisive point when I remembered a passage from the Rule of Saint Benedict, a little fifteen-hundred-year-old book by the founder of the Benedictine order, with a sentence that said, 'Have death at all times before your eyes.' With the war over and my life ahead of me, I suddenly remembered how we had been so happy being forced to live in the present moment with death at all times before our eyes."

The experience of the war in his youth, combined with the teachings of Saint Benedict, sparked Brother David's desire to pursue a life of monastic contemplation and study. But he was never one to see monasticism as a passive or reclusive existence. He began to travel the world as an ambassador for interfaith dialogue and as an activist alongside Thich Nhat Hanh and other spiritual luminaries. From a depth of knowledge nurtured within the monastic tradition and a rich outer life rooted in the everyday world, Brother David dug deep to the center of poignant universal truths and has blessed the world with his resonant and accessible scholarship. The centerpiece of his explorations has always been gratefulness, a quality he asserts is at the very heart of prayer, happiness, and a world at peace.

In 2000, Brother David and a few close friends founded A Network for Grateful Living. The original purpose of the nonprofit organization was to create an Internet platform to share Brother David's teachings about gratefulness and to offer inspiration for the growing global community of people interested in "online support for offline living." The website was loaded with tools and features to uplift the practice of grateful living, and offered a monthly newsletter and Word for the Day email with an inspiring quote for contemplation. After meeting Brother David, I subscribed.

The Call

Brother David and I had the shared experience of facing death and surviving, and the subsequent challenge of finding a path that would support and sustain a posture of gratefulness toward life. Brother David went the way of monasticism. I went the way of nonprofit leadership in organizations focused on personal and societal transformation. We found one another and our deep common ground in the commitment to living gratefully, and all the gifts that flow from it.

In January 2014, I learned that A Network for Grateful Living was searching for a new executive director. I was not looking for work at the time, but when I read the job posting, I felt as if I could check off every one of the skills and strengths they were seeking. I sensed serendipity in the air. The interview process involved a teleconference with Brother David. I was thrilled to see him again and, ultimately, to be chosen by the board for the position I am thankful to have held these many years.

While *gratefulness* and *grateful living* are terms Brother David has successfully brought into greater awareness, I began to feel that we needed to be able to offer a stronger example and articulation of grateful living as a day-to-day practice. When people would ask me about the steps involved in living gratefully, I had little to offer aside from Brother David's advice to simply *Stop. Look. Go.* This advice sounds wonderful coming from an endearing 93-year-old Benedictine monk with a twinkle in his eye and one of the best accents in the world. But it was far less compelling coming from me, and I struggled with how to make the practice of grateful living more understandable and actionable.

So, with encouragement and support from everyone at A Network for Grateful Living, I set out to write a book articulating a framework based on Brother David's teachings that would make the gifts of grateful living accessible and relevant to the widest possible audience. I wanted to make grateful living readily available and resonant to you.

The Book

Wake Up Grateful is a guidebook — plus a whole lot more. It is a framework for transforming your life and the world around you. It's a book you can pick up any day and open to any page and find a nugget of wisdom, a quote, practice, or question that will leave you more reflective and resourceful in bringing gratitude into your life. It holds a personal story that offers hope. It is a source of inspiration and guidance for everyday life and for specific areas of life where it is common to struggle. Navigate at your own pace and notice which lessons speak most directly to you and which elements work best for the circumstances of your life. It is a process of continually reminding yourself to return again and again to what matters.

A grateful life is made up of grateful days, and grateful days are made up of grateful moments. This book is meant to point you toward a way of life that will bring you more of these moments and experiences. You can personalize the practices and tools and apply them to challenges as they arise. Reflection questions may inspire insightful time with your own journal. Some of your explorations may be solitary, and some may be strengthened in relationship. You may want to use this book with your family, partner, or friends, or start a group in your community. You can find Grateful Living Groups around the world at Grateful.org, where you will also find an abundance of additional resources to support your continued practice and exploration.

I explain in Part 1 what I see as grateful living's Five Guiding Principles: *Life Is a Gift, Everything Is Surprise, The Ordinary Is Extraordinary, Appreciation Is Generative,* and *Love Is Transformative.* These principles are touchstones you can turn to at any time and in any situation to remind you of what matters most in living gratefully. We will also explore and expand on Brother David's practice of *Stop. Look. Go.*, including Five Points of Perspective for the times when you need them: embrace poignancy, invite peak awareness, acknowledge privilege and plenty, align with your principles, and open to pleasure.

Part II focuses on how you can bring grateful living practice into specific areas of life that call for deeper attention, and where it may be able to serve you the most. I will examine ten areas where many of us often need support: uncertainty, the body, emotions, ourselves, relationships, loss, nature, contentment, our world, and legacy. Finding presence and perspective in these aspects of our lives is what helps to open up a sense of possibility. I have chosen to share my personal cancer story, as well as the voices of people who have been practicing grateful living in the face of these sorts of challenges, and a favorite poem in each chapter. My hope is to deepen a sense of relatedness so that greater resonance and possibility are awakened in you.

The Path

I believe that if you are a seeker and your heart is moved by what is true and what is possible, then you will be drawn to the path of grateful living. Look for those who are easily moved, and you will likely find the most grateful people. Moved by grief. Moved by beauty. Moved by hope. Look for those who have the capacity to let themselves be rocked by the magnificence and hardship of life as it is, and you will find people for whom gratefulness is a way of being.

Grateful living offers a path and a promise. It is an intimate orientation to life. The more gratefully and intimately we dare to approach and engage with life, the more intimately we will experience it, and everything it has to offer. The more we befriend and acknowledge vulnerability, uncertainty, and imper-manence, the more appreciative and alive we become. Grateful living rests in this paradox. When we are awake, we experience this paradox and its gifts every day.

The path of grateful living is one that activates our hearts and lives toward love. Grateful living gives our hearts wide wings and stamina for the journey because it is grounded in all that is real and based in life as it is. It supports us to be moved and impacted — fully present for the opportunities of our lives, our relationships, and the larger world to which we belong. Grateful living allows us to show up for life, and then it sticks with us unconditionally — whether we feel gratitude or not, whether we are happy or not. It hangs around as we go through the great fullness of life, offering its radically gracious presence.

May this book offer you a deep well from which to drink and nourishment for the journey, and may your heart overflow into blessing every day — within you, and all around you.

PART I

FROM GRATITUDE
TO
GRATEFUL LIVING

CHAPTER 1

GRATEFULNESS
Gratitude for the Great Fullness of Life

It is not happiness that makes us grateful.
It is gratefulness that makes us happy.
BROTHER DAVID STEINDL-RAST

＊

Gratitude is great. When we receive something we want, when experiences bring us pleasure, or when life goes our way, it is natural and meaningful to feel gratitude. Gratitude is like a magic potion that we can sprinkle on a wilted plant to bring it back to life. Sprinkled on a relationship, it does the same. Scattered throughout a day, it leaves us and those in our path happier. Scientific studies continue to reveal that gratitude is simply good medicine, for us and for others. When we feel grateful we are happier, healthier, kinder, more generous, more satisfied, and more resilient.

Most of us would like to feel grateful far more often. But how? How can you experience gratitude when life gets challenging? What can help you sustain the experience of being grateful without needing life to be other than it is, or without wanting more from the people and world around you? How can you navigate the stumbling blocks that keep you from being grateful even when you want to be, or know you should be?

Imagine being able to have gratitude that is unconditional and lasting. A gratitude that does not depend on what happens, but comes from the inside out. Not a reaction to something, but a proactive approach to life. A gratitude already with you as you wake to greet your days — before anything has even happened. This is gratefulness. As the connective tissue between our moments and experiences, gratefulness allows us to find gratitude in the "great fullness" of life in all its real-world moments of messiness and magnificence.

GRATITUDE IS GREAT; GRATEFULNESS IS GREATER

To speak about the differences between gratitude and gratefulness might seem like quibbling over semantics, but there are important distinctions. The common understanding of the word *gratitude* simply does not convey the magnitude of gratefulness and all that it offers us as a way of being in the world. Gratefulness does not reserve itself only for when good things happen or we get what we want. It is more than simply saying thank you when things go well or counting your blessings at the end of the day. Gratefulness revels in the deeper truths of "I woke up again today" or "I can still notice beauty after another hard day." It enables us to have the tenacity to attend and respond in a more resilient way to our challenges. It is a perspective shift to: *No matter what happens, I still know that every moment offers me something for which to feel thankful, and I make myself available to the exploration.* Gratefulness opens us to the opportunity to experience gratitude in every moment.

Gratefulness is gratitude for life. It reminds us that, in simply being alive, we are always receiving. While gratitude — as we know it — needs something good to happen, gratefulness only needs us to be awake. We do not need to *do* anything to feel grateful, or wait for anything more. We merely need to allow ourselves to notice and be wowed by things we so often overlook and tend to take for granted in the lives we already have.

GRATEFULNESS AS A WAY OF BEING

We are all moving through life guided by our attention and our intentions. Gratefulness is a *way of being* that helps us to focus our attention and navigate our lives with gratitude as our compass. Consider all the forces that have conspired effectively for you to be here right now reading these words. Your presence is the result of millions of things not going wrong, and millions of things working perfectly. With a grateful orientation, we bring awareness to all that is miraculous about life and awaken to the opportunities in every moment.

We all deal with moments and experiences that cause us to feel disconnected and disoriented. Life will knock us off course in any number of ways: unexpected bad news, our own suffering and that of others, abrupt change, loss. Small daily disappointments, heartaches, and tensions can also disorient us. Successfully navigating life in its fullness calls for resilience — orienting yourself in a way that can help you meet and greet whatever unfolds. As a way of being, gratefulness can offer a compass and trail markers to help you find your way back to a state of well-being whenever you lose your way. Gratefulness becomes your true North.

✳

How could the distinctions between gratitude and gratefulness
help you be aware of more opportunities in your life?

✳

With gratefulness as an orientation to life, what makes you
feel grateful right now?

A FISH IN WATER

When you are a fish, it must be hard to describe water. That is how it can feel trying to explain gratefulness sometimes. It's a bit like trying to find the words to explain grief or joy. It is big and unwieldy. Sometimes my body wants to describe it: the ways that gratefulness animates the cells, activates the heart, settles my monkey mind. I could say how being grateful wakes me up in the morning and puts me to sleep at night. How it can make me more intolerant of injustice and more passionate about love, both always with greater hope. But mostly, it helps me to appreciate the opportunities nestled inside every stressful moment, and to notice trust peeking around the edges of all my fears. Gratefulness brings me perspective and reminds me of the privileges and opportunities of my life. It helps me navigate choppy waters and better enjoy riding the waves. It has become inextricable from who I am. Kind of like a fish and water — it gives me life.

EMBRACING THE GREAT FULLNESS OF LIFE

Gratefulness helps you to embrace the entirety of your experience. It helps you to learn from life as it actually is — with nothing left out, either beautiful or painful. It opens us to the teachings and opportunities within every moment. It offers us what we need not merely to survive difficult times but to appreciate their gifts, even when the gifts take time to reveal themselves. When life feels too small or too big to handle, too predictable or too uncertain, this is when we need gratefulness most.

It is not the intention of gratefulness to make the suffering of life become worthy of praise. We cannot be grateful for everything that happens. Instead, through a grateful orientation, we can learn to feel grateful in every moment, and better able to recognize and seize opportunities for learning, insight, love, and action in the midst of our challenges. Gratefulness is an activator, not a pacifier. To acknowledge that something is true does not mean that it is acceptable, but we can only respond effectively once we see clearly what is happening. The more we are in touch with the great fullness of life, the more we can respond with great fullness of heart.

As we allow gratefulness to guide us, we recognize an expanded ability to trust ourselves and to trust life as it unfolds. In challenging moments, we remember that painful experiences have taught us courage. Greater joy and freedom have been earned in being with life as it is. We remember that it is possible to emerge from our difficulties with compassion for ourselves and others. There are certainly times that gratefulness will feel like a stretch. But life often stretches us as we develop our capacity to meet what arrives in our days and hearts. Gratefulness helps us to build this capacity.

LIFE IS EVERYTHING; EVERYTHING IS LIFE

Our lives can often feel very full, too full. While this fullness is something we might begrudge, it also reflects privilege and good fortune if regarded differently. What would it take to see the commitments and responsibilities in our lives as blessings and privileges? What can we do to remember our good fortune in having people and things to consider and tend? Imagine losing or not having access to those things that sometimes feel burdensome — a home, chores, loved ones, your car, your job. Many people do not have the gift of the choices or concerns we have. The privilege to consider and be considered — this may be our greatest wealth. Gratefulness helps us savor these riches and opportunities.

✳

In what ways could you bring greater fullness of heart to the fullness of your life?

✳

What are some obligations or responsibilities in your life you would like to feel more grateful about?

PRACTICE
From Obligation to Opportunity

Write a list of at least five things that you have to do this week. Your responsibilities, your to-do list. Begin each item with the words "I have to . . ." For example: I have to pay bills. I have to go grocery shopping. I have to go to the dentist. I have to make that overdue phone call. I have to prepare for a meeting. I have to do laundry. I have to fix the kitchen light. I have to pick up my kids.

Now cross out the words "I have to" and begin each line with the words "I get to." Notice how different it feels to think that you *get* to do something. How does this shift the energy you bring to each task?

Throughout your day, catch yourself whenever you think, "I have to . . ." and try to substitute with "I get to." You can also try adding, "because I can" to the end of your "get-to" statements. This can help you see your tasks as privileges you may not have always had and may not always have in the future, and that many people do not have at all. Begin to notice how much other people use obligated language in day-to-day conversations. Experiment with seeing and claiming your responsibilities and obligations as privileges and opportunities.

INHIBITORS TO GRATEFULNESS

Brother David Steindl-Rast is renowned for saying, "It is not happiness that makes us grateful. It is gratefulness that makes us happy." We can have all the things we think *should* bring us happiness, but without gratefulness, contentment will be elusive. With our projections and expectations in charge, the grass will always seem greener on the other side of the fence. At least until we are grateful for the grass we have.

There are many factors that can inhibit or overwhelm our ability to feel grateful. Some of these forces are learned and reinforced in the culture at large; others live at the personal level. We might experience many inhibitors in a given day or interaction, but they can be addressed with awareness and intention.

Assumptions and Expectations

I thought it was going to be different from this.

When we walk into a situation that we think will go a certain way, and then it does not go as we expected, it is hard to rise above our disappointment to notice the good that did unfold. Our thoughts about how things should or will happen inhibit our ability to be grateful for what is.

An expectation is something that you want to happen, but you are not sure will. An assumption is something you think will happen, and you are almost sure will. Left unchecked, expectations and assumptions that go wrong lead to anger or regret, sadness or disappointment.

Comparison and Jealousy

I would be grateful if I had what they have.

Theodore Roosevelt said, "Comparison is the thief of joy." Comparison is one of those insidious habits that can be destructive to gratefulness. It is so common and automatic to compare ourselves to people who seem to have more than we do that we are hard-pressed to be aware of the ways comparison carries us down a road of discontentment. Feelings that hitch themselves to comparison are jealousy, envy, and covetousness, which leave us feeling "less than" and thinking we never have, or are, enough.

Scarcity and Insatiability

I need more in order to feel grateful.

Living within an economic system fueled by endless consumption, it is easy to understand why a sense of scarcity is so pervasive. This is the feeling of not having enough, rather than the truth of not having our basic needs met.

Felt-scarcity can motivate insatiable behavior regardless of how much we do or do not have. Insatiability is one of the great inhibitors to gratefulness. As long as you come from the belief that more, better, and different are the necessities of a happy life, your efforts to feel grateful will keep you coming up empty.

Entitlement

I deserve this, and more.

If we walk through our days with an elevated level of deservingness — as though life, with all its moments and inhabitants, is on the hook for providing us what we want and need at all times — satisfaction and gratitude will be hard to come by. Feeling that life must unfold in particular ways that will please us is a recipe for loss of humility and connection. Entitlement can often look like arrogance. It is also the sibling of greed. The underbelly of entitlement is often an inferiority complex. None of this makes it easy to feel gratified or grateful.

Invulnerability

I do not want to owe anyone anything.

Gratefulness relies on our ability to value interdependence and vulnerability. We will find ourselves lacking without a deep regard for the contributions of others to our lives. We are awakened to gratefulness when we recognize the countless contributions of others on whom we rely and depend in the course of our daily lives. This recognition is humbling. Going through life thick-skinned and protected by bravado will keep us from experiencing and expressing appreciation for our tender ties to one another.

✳

In what areas of life do you find that assumptions or expectations diminish your capacity to appreciate what actually unfolds in your life?

✳

In what areas of your life are you most susceptible to comparison, scarcity, entitlement, or invulnerability? How does this keep you from feeling grateful?

THE WISDOM OF GRATEFULNESS

When we are grateful, it wakes us up to what matters. It helps us be aware of all that is sufficient and abundant in our lives. It keeps us alert to meaningful truths. It supports our capacity to live with appreciation, and it makes us more alive.

Throughout this unpredictable blessing called life, gratefulness helps us to be awake, aware, alert, appreciative, and alive. These are the attributes of an intentional life, and the states of consciousness that foster insight and wisdom, necessary in leading the life we want to live now and *have lived* in the end. It is in how we live our moments today that we will live a lifetime that matters.

Awake to What Matters

Normal day, let me be aware of the treasure you are. Let me learn from you, love you, savor you, bless you before you depart. Let me not pass you by in quest of some rare and perfect tomorrow. — Mary Jean Irion

Gratefulness helps us be awake to what matters, and to not sleepwalk our way through life. One of the most important reasons to live with gratefulness is that it keeps us connected with our deepest cares, greatest blessings, and true priorities without needing a dramatic wake-up call to remind us of them.

We've all had these kinds of warning experiences: the close call on the road, a health scare, loss of a loved one. Wouldn't it be a blessing if we did not need the threat of loss in order to appreciate the gifts and advantages we already have? Rather than rely on alarming experiences to wake us up to what we treasure, we can cultivate a state of being awake and grateful and not miss the opportunities our lives offer us every day.

The wisdom of gratefulness rests on the opportunity to actively appreciate what you have now. You make the choice to act with a grateful heart now, knowing that you do not want to wait for a wake-up call, or wait until it is too late.

＊

How could being more awake to what you appreciate serve your life?

＊

What matters to you that you want to tend gratefully now without needing a wake-up call to remind you?

Aware of Enough

*How many of us go through our days parched and empty, thirsting
after happiness, when we're really standing knee-deep in the river of
abundance?* — Sarah Ban Breathnach

It is easy to feel overwhelmed by the pace of our days, the demands of increasingly complex lives, media messaging, the push to consume, the pull to compare and crave, and the feeling that we never are or have enough. All of this steals the extraordinary from the ordinary, and makes us lose sight of our blessings and take what we have for granted.

Gratefulness is a powerful intervention whenever a sense of lack permeates our lives. We could spend our days awestruck and thankful about how much of the extraordinary we already have going for us. But when what we want is positioned as something just beyond our reach — one purchase, one person, one possibility away from what is ours — we have to work hard to maintain contentment.

As *The Soul of Money* author Lynne Twist says, when we are caught on the treadmill rushing toward more, we barrel right past "enough" as if it were nothing more than an inconvenient speed bump. Contentment is a blessing begging for our recognition, but we are unaccustomed to pausing long enough to see how much it offers. To maintain an awareness of what is already extraordinary and abundant in our lives is a satisfaction that cannot be taken away.

Gratefulness opens us to the experience of enough. Suddenly, the corners of our homes are rich with items for which to be thankful. What seemed lacking in our relationship now feels abundant. Our bodies are miraculous. Electricity blows our minds. The Earth is an endless symphony of beauty.

Living gratefully establishes the conditions not only for deeper happiness but also for generosity and the impulse to serve others. When we are awake to all that is enough in our lives, we more readily turn our attention beyond ourselves. We need to feel our own fullness in order to offer what is meaningful to others.

✴

What are some of the extraordinary aspects of your life *as it is* that
you tend to overlook? How could you be more aware of them?

✴

What do you have enough of? What is already more than enough in your life?

Alert to Life Itself

Alertness is the hidden discipline of familiarity. — David Whyte

Through the lens of gratefulness, the proverbial glass half-full, glass half-empty story moves beyond optimism or pessimism. We are able to see a new story, with a new perspective, about the privilege of having a glass at all. The glass is the gift of your life. Noticing and being grateful for this container helps to turn its contents — whatever is in there and however much — in your favor. To be grateful for having a glass is key because, without it, half of anything wouldn't matter! It is easy to spend our lives in an attempt to change our circumstances from having less to having more, but focusing on things that come and go just keeps us in a relentless pursuit of even more.

Gratefulness is about knowing in your bones that each day is precious. It also acknowledges the inevitability of change. One moment we can feel empty, and the next moment full. One moment life offers us only a trickle, and at other times it overflows. If you learn to connect with the privileges of your life, knowing you are "held" by a container that feels brimming even as the water level perpetually changes, that is the experience of true good fortune.

✸

How could you shift some of your conversations toward the gift of the glass itself rather than focusing on whether it is half-full or half-empty?

✸

When you think more about having a glass and less about what is in it, how does it change your perspective on your life right now?

Appreciation for Ourselves

Happiness is to appreciate what you have; unhappiness is to dwell on what you don't have. — Rabbi Shimon Ben Zoma

We can sometimes stumble through our lives half-asleep. When we feel blue or anxious, our daily experiences only seem to reinforce that feeling. As stuck as we might feel, there are ways to shift our experience if we turn our attention toward appreciation, especially appreciation for ourselves. Everything flourishes in the nourishment of our appreciation. When you live with appreciation, *you* flourish.

Appreciation invites you to fold yourself into the field of your own tender attention the way you would extend yourself to any other beloved person. You commit to lifelong curiosity and interest. You delight in discovering and naming your quirks and idiosyncrasies. You offer empathy for your vulnerabilities. You practice beholding rather than belittling, befriending rather than begrudging. You choose to love your body and offer it the healing that the outside world can never provide. You hold yourself as you want to be held and feel yourself held in the grand embrace of belonging.

Gratefulness reminds us that we do not need to do, have, or be anything different to be worthy of our own appreciation. You do not have to change in any way to deserve your own care. Instead, you can extend a more merciful acceptance for every aspect of who you are, exactly as you are. When appreciation guides our relationship to ourselves and we feel self-compassion, this provides us a frame of reference to better appreciate and feel compassion for others too.

✳

What parts of you await your unconditional, tender appreciation?

✳

What changes might be unleashed in your life if you were to befriend yourself more fully?

Alive to Joy

Joy is not a luxury, it is not a privilege. It is a resilience-giving, life-giving birthright and we can't call forth in the world something we don't believe in and embody. — Krista Tippett

Both joy and gratefulness are unconditional, deeply rooted, and tenacious enough to coexist with the difficulties of our lives. Brother David says, "Joy is the happiness that does not depend on what happens." Joy is often hiding just underneath or behind something else. It is revealed through curiosity and wonder. It is lurking inside simple moments that beg for your greater presence and appreciation. When you tap into a grateful heart, you are connecting with the same forces that help you to experience this joy. It is our full aliveness that wakes up the presence of joy. It is in learning to embrace and appreciate the fullness of your life as it is that joy emerges.

Gratefulness, joy, and aliveness are a self-fulfilling cycle, each nourishing and compelling the other. This cycle not only animates us as individuals, it emboldens the life-force of love, which will ripple out to positively impact others in our life. Living gratefully fills our hearts to overflowing, and love makes our hearts spill over into generosity.

✳

What does it mean to you to cultivate greater aliveness? How might this connect you to joy?

✳

What are some of the ways you can prioritize and nurture what enlivens you?

SCALING JOY

I love holding the intention of inviting more aliveness into my days. It is one of those slightly bewildering but energizing aspirations. My mind wants me to settle for "You're already alive," but the rest of me knows well that we experience aliveness on a scale — kind of like awakeness. In my longing to be fully awake, I know it does not serve me to settle for the lower registers. What makes me more alive? What is sacred to me: Nature. Love. Light. Poetry. Especially when I get to experience them all at the same time. Love for nature and the nature of love, love of light and the light of love, and the essential poetry of it all. And of course the more grateful I am for all the things that inspire this aliveness, the more I am in touch with deep joy. What an exquisite incentive. Having a moment-to-moment practice that reminds me to be grateful for life helps to tip the scales in favor of everything that matters to me.

FROM GRATEFULNESS TO GRATEFUL LIVING

When we live gratefully, gratefulness comes to life. We do not have to be grateful for everything that happens, but learning how to be grateful in every moment — even and especially in the great fullness of life — is supported by trustworthy principles.

CHAPTER 2

GRATEFUL LIVING AS A WAY OF LIFE
Five Guiding Principles

Speaking of grateful living is another way of speaking about full aliveness, and waking up to the joy of life.
BROTHER DAVID STEINDL-RAST

✳

Grateful living brings the abundant gifts of gratitude to life. When we live gratefully, all of our moments, choices, and interactions can be impacted. As a *way of life*, grateful living helps us to navigate everything that unfolds in our days. It is a trustworthy road map even in our most challenging times. We find ourselves pausing to be present and gain perspective when we used to simply push ahead. We find ourselves wondering in the middle of feeling beleaguered, "What is the opportunity here, right now?" We act from a greater sense of sufficiency rather than deficiency and offer our gifts freely where they are needed. We are generous with our appreciation, which adds magic to our relationships. Gratefully engaged with the moment at hand, we find an unexpected doorway into well-being and joy.

THE FIVE GUIDING PRINCIPLES

Brother David's teachings on gratefulness encompass Five Guiding Principles. These principles are a support structure for you to lean on whenever you find yourself approaching a moment or opportunity and want to do so wholeheartedly. They offer a comforting and catalyzing reference point for your thoughts and actions, and a continual reminder of guiding truths.

You can connect with the Five Guiding Principles as a way of welcoming and acting from gratefulness in your daily life. Each one has a wealth of support to offer, and on its own is powerful enough to transform your life if you dive deeply into its invitation and offerings. Taken together, they are a robust practice in support of deeper well-being and greater joy, and they build on one another in a trustworthy progression. These are the five touchstones you can return to as wisdom in your daily life: *Life Is a Gift, Everything Is Surprise, The Ordinary Is Extraordinary, Appreciation Is Generative,* and *Love Is Transformative.*

1. LIFE IS A GIFT

This is a wonderful day. I've never seen this one before. — Maya Angelou

Grateful living is fundamentally grounded in the invitation to see life itself as a gift: an unexpected gift that you did not need to do anything to earn or deserve, but is coming to you — wrapped in a wide range of packaging. In every moment that you are alive, this life has been given to you.

So often we walk through our days feeling that there is something missing, and that we need more. We may not know exactly what that *more* is, but we know we long to feel filled up and fully alive. We want to be connected to what really matters. We want to belong. And we want to feel chosen. And yet, during all of these moments, there is life again holding its steady commitment out to us. Offering yet another moment. Another opportunity. Life keeps on extending itself, even when we walk past it waiting for a better invitation, something wrapped in different paper or a bigger box.

With perspective, you see life as an extraordinary privilege, and one not to squander. It is the gift that brings everything else with it. And in every moment it awaits your engagement. Accepting this invitation, you become a partner with your unfolding moments in creating the unrepeatable miracle that is, in the words of poet Mary Oliver, "your one wild and precious life."

Grateful living reminds us that by seeing life as a gift we acquire a consistent and sufficient baseline for gratefulness. It is the beginning, and will be the end, of the most powerful practice we have. Life itself is our most reliable cause for gratefulness. We honor life with our wholehearted presence and appreciation by repeatedly saying *yes* to the gift that it is.

Greet Each Moment Gratefully

We have the opportunity to enliven our moments by how we greet them. They are arriving in an ever-steady stream, so greeting each moment gratefully could keep us very, very busy, but it is worth doing! As you practice grateful living, you discover greater presence for life's unfolding. This presence does not require us to consistently re-up and double-check our commitment. When we live gratefully, we have the opportunity to return again and again to the moment at hand, seeing it as our good fortune, and we only need offer it our awareness and acknowledgment.

You Are Always Receiving

When we think of life as a gift, we can fully trust that as long as we are breathing, we are receiving. Tuning into the miracle of our breath and bodies at any moment is a baseline reminder. We wake up to notice the unconditional gifts and opportunities available to us in each "uneventful" moment, and we can enter that awakened state at any time. No matter how we might be struggling, there are always ways to focus our attention on what we are receiving and what is working in service of our lives. It is often a matter of intentionally shifting our attention away from the pull of what is missing to notice more fully all that is present. This shift in perspective helps us remember how filled up and fortunate we are. Turning our attention toward the steady stream of gifts that life is casting your way can help you tap into the sweetness of sufficiency, and awe for the sources of your abundance.

PRACTICES
Wake Up Grateful

When you wake up, before getting out of bed, pause to notice and appreciate at least three things you can already be grateful for. For example: I am alive. My lungs are working. My eyes can open. My body can move. There are people I love. I had a dream. I can feel the air on my skin. I am part of the human family. Think of things that you do not have to do anything to earn or receive from anyone else — things you are already receiving from life before doing anything. This is a powerful practice to greet each day and helps you to feel centered in the privilege and gifts of life.

Inside-Out

Turn your attention inward toward awareness of what you are receiving right now from inside your body. Notice your breath and feel it as life-giving. Feel your heart pumping and how it enlivens you. Tune in to some of the other sophisticated systems in your body that are operating to support your life. The continual functioning of your body is one of the most basic, ever-available miracles there is. Let it continually amaze you.

Outside-In

Notice how much you are receiving from the world around you. Remind yourself of gravity as a gift that literally keeps you grounded. Think of the air flowing into your lungs as "inspiration." Appreciate the current time of day and weather. Consider the many people involved in keeping electricity, running water, and communication with the world available for you. No matter who or where you are, no matter your circumstances, you can always be grateful for these blessings. Let them move you.

Insight-Full

When we quiet the voices and noise inside and around us, we can tune in to wise guidance that is always available. Create a regular practice to tune in to your own core intelligence, the wellspring that manifests as heart guidance, gut instinct, and intuition. There is endless wisdom waiting for you in every moment, so you are able to receive it endlessly. It is a surefire path to connecting with awe for the great fullness of life.

✳

Coming to stillness, what are some of the gifts that you are aware of receiving in this moment?

✳

What are some ways you can remind yourself to greet your moments more fully and gratefully?

FAITHFUL MIRACLES

I am most deeply moved and supported by gratefulness when I bring to mind the ordinary blessings that are ever-available to me no matter how many material goods I have, how connected I feel to others, or how healthy, comfortable, or mobile I am. Focusing on the things I am always receiving points me to that which is truly unconditional and most faithful. The miracles of my breath, my heartbeat, my senses, the sky, the Earth. If I quiet myself sufficiently, I can access the gifts of inner and outer guidance, instinct, intuition. Even if I do not feel directly connected to them in the moment myself, the existence of courage, beauty, creativity, love, the resilience of the human spirit . . . these awaken me to hope. It is the consistent presence of the miraculous inside the ordinary that helps me most, especially when I am in touch with life's unpredictability. Remembering the faithfulness of the basic gifts of life is what comforts me. Even in the very last moments of my life, I know with certainty that this will be my path to a grateful heart.

2. EVERYTHING IS SURPRISE

Surprise is the greatest gift which life can grant us. — Boris Pasternak

When you regard life as an unexpected gift and one you are lucky to have renew itself each day, it can shift your experience of expectation. Freed from expectations, you learn to not simply experience life as you think it will be and as it has always been, but are curious and intrigued to discover the inevitably surprising things life has in store for you next. Without the habitual ways of perceiving your life, you can embrace uncertainty and notice things as babies do, as travelers visiting a foreign country, or with the awakened senses of someone told they only have weeks to live. You can behold life with the openness of experiencing things as if for the very first, or the very last, time. Guided by this principle, you trust that life will always be a surprise.

Being open to surprise is an antidote to a life lived on autopilot. Nothing surprising will come from projecting what we think we know. It does not come from anticipating the same-old same-old. It comes from the unforeseen. We need to be relieved of our propensity to think that life is within the white-knuckled purview of our control. With fewer efforts to predict and control, more of life emerges as itself, and with that will come both delight and difficulty. If we try to control everything, we may screen out some difficulty, but we will inevitably screen out delight, too.

As we become more present, surprise will accompany us on what was formerly a mind-numbing commute to work, or a routine trip up and down the aisles of a grocery store. We are alert to appreciation as we weren't before, and the old becomes new again. Textures and complexities suddenly surface and beckon amazement. We notice things in sharp relief, as if we have not seen them before: colors, sounds, feelings, sensations. Once set on this new path, we find that everything and everyone we thought we knew begins to surprise us: weather, foods, neighbors, words. Even ourselves.

Open to Wonder

When we are available for unencumbered encounters with life, we see that there is a lot more going on, and a lot more possible, than our limited capacities and interests can fathom. One of the great enemies of learning is "knowing." To greet life with curiosity and wonder is to value surprise. Curiosity is a willingness to learn anew, to be changed, shaken out of our comfort zones. A state of wonder opens us to new ways of seeing, and delivers us space for discovery and inquisitiveness. We spend great reserves of energy and resources orchestrating elaborate enjoyable experiences, and all the while things are happening around us that can offer greater pleasure than we could ever coordinate. Look up — shooting stars. Look down — heart-shaped stones. Look around — faces with stories they are longing to tell. We all have room for discovery, and grateful living is the doorway that opens to it.

Opportunities Abound

Openness to surprise delivers on the big promise of grateful living: awareness of opportunity. When we live gratefully, we open all our senses toward opportunities, aware that they are always there, no matter our circumstances. We become surprised to discover opportunities between, behind, and around the things to which we have become accustomed. It is we who need to lean in, listen for them, and follow their invitations. The process of continually waking up points us to live more gratefully, with each opportunity seen as the chance to notice and appreciate the gifts in our midst, and each moment we are alive as the chance to truly live.

PRACTICES
Doing It Differently

When you are in the midst of a routine, stop for one minute to bring greater awareness to what you are doing. First, notice when you are doing something habitually. To do this same activity gratefully requires greater presence. Bring attention to your task and change one aspect so it comes more alive, and you do, too. Switch hands when brushing your teeth. Swap your usual seat at the table. Sleep on a different side of the bed, or in a different room. Take a new route to work. Try expressing generous thanks to someone you see every day. Changing a habit changes perspective, making room for new awareness. Let yourself feel the awkwardness and delight of something different. See what kinds of insights and opportunities arise when you become open to surprise.

Gift Reminders

It can help you appreciate your life more when you imagine not having the things to which you are accustomed. Expectations keep us asleep to life; surprise wakes us up. Cultivating a state of astonishment about your many comforts — running water, a laptop, a coffeemaker, a refrigerator, a window, or even a roof over your head — helps keep you grateful. How would life be without these privileges? Put a sticker or even a small gift bow — yes, really — on things you want to remind yourself not to forget are surprising gifts. This can also help others in your household or workplace treat things as amazing blessings rather than the same old things.

Natural Inspiration

Whenever possible, get yourself outside. Invite your senses to open wider, and wonder will always find you. Let yourself follow where it leads. Opportunities will reveal themselves. Take risks to make yourself available to the gifts of amazement. Go out under the night sky when you cannot sleep. Set an alarm to see the sun rise every morning for a week. Befriend a tree and notice its changes every day. Plant something, or plant yourself somewhere on the land for an hour and notice how life teems around you. Our Earth waits for you with abundant surprise. Make yourself available.

✳

What is the surprising truth of life inviting you to notice right now?

✳

What opportunity is beckoning for your attention?

THE PATH OF A WONDERER

Surprise wants me to slow down. To change my pace and make a little space to welcome it into my days. To stop having so many of my moments planned and filled. Surprise wants me to stop expecting so much and let myself actually experience more. It wants me to roll out the red carpet for whatever comes in life, instead of being so fixated on what I hope will happen, what I *want* to happen. Surprise says, "If you live with the open heart and eyes of a child, I will accompany you. Yes, you will scrape your knees, but you will know much more about delight. Delight is what I deliver into the space in the heart you have been cluttering with the expectations you have mistaken for adulthood. You have left me so little room. Surrender to me. Let's play. I come bearing infinite gifts." Surprise wants me to be less afraid, pick up more stones and look underneath them, venture out into all kinds of weather, ponder questions a little longer, reach out to strangers, and dare to call wonder my home.

3. THE ORDINARY IS EXTRAORDINARY

*Some people have a wonderful capacity to appreciate again and again,
freshly and naively, the basic goods of life, with awe, pleasure, wonder,
and even ecstasy.* — Abraham Maslow

One of the most accessible and direct pathways to a sense of abundance —
after the recognition that life is always bestowing the gift of itself on you — is
to savor and celebrate the ordinary. How can you experience the generosity of
your life more vividly and more consistently? How can you feel overflowing
with good fortune, even in the midst of real or felt scarcity? *Ordinary* may
simply be the label that we put on something we have neglected to appreciate
or have come to take for granted — something or someone we walk by or benefit from every day without acknowledgment, curiosity, or celebration.

What is truly ordinary anyway? Is there such a thing as an ordinary flower?
Sunrise? Book? Bird? Are there ordinary days? Movies? Music? Conversations?
Meals? How would people from other cultures regard what we think of as
run-of-the-mill? How about our great-grandparents? The things we scurry
past might stop them in their tracks. And what about us, 20 or 30 years ago?
Our current *ordinary* would have been an unimaginable extraordinary to our
younger selves. Always, the vantage point of a distant observer helps expand
our awareness. As does the cultivation of awe and appreciation.

Take Nothing for Granted

The 180-degree opposite of gratefulness is to take life for granted. It is the death
knell to a satisfying and joyful life. If you want the most basic instruction in
how to live gratefully, it would be to stop taking people, possessions, your body,
time — literally anything — for granted. Put in positive terms, actively treasuring whatever is yours to treasure is the shortest path to joy you can take.

Committing to taking nothing for granted is an ambitious daily practice.
"Nothing" is a lot. One thing each day acknowledged and appreciated that
we previously overlooked — that is enough. These commitments are like the
chime after the snooze button, a reminder to wake up and not let life pass us
by. Or not walk past the extraordinary people we love, relegating them to the
ordinary. Or even expect them to always be there, right where we left them.

Life Is Abundant

When you see the ordinary as extraordinary and take nothing for granted, this alone can turn your life into a treasure trove. If you look at everything with appreciative eyes, you are likely to be overwhelmed by the amazing gifts at your fingertips, the abundance of how much is in service to your life. Awakening to the great good fortune that is ours can put the kibosh on our feeling of needing "more." The practice of fully appreciating what is already in front of us can be a joyful long-term engagement. You might be surprised as you begin this practice to find that you already have all the abundance that you envied, craved, or thought you needed to get something.

PRACTICES

Well-Served

Throughout your day, as you come into contact with any item you typically treat as ordinary — a toothbrush, fork, pillow, pen — pause for a few moments to allow it to reveal its extraordinariness. Consider the enjoyment it gives, the service it provides, the activities it allows. Consider its beauty and ingenuity. Imagine what a blessing it might be to many people just to have this ordinary item in their life. Imagine what your life might be like without it. Care for its extraordinariness with appropriate reverence. Create a ritual of pausing with appreciation before you drive your car, or use your computer. Savor one moment to acknowledge the privileges that your commonplace luxuries afford you.

Parts of the Whole

Try regularly regarding any object you might otherwise take for granted with curious consideration. As you hold a book, sip a cup of tea, arrange a meal on a plate, sit under the light of a lamp, think about how you came to have this item in your life. What went into making it? How many different people might have been involved in bringing it into the world? How was it transported? What forces had to collaborate to bring it into being? Think of all the human, earthly, and other ecosystems involved in bringing you this gift. Keep being curious. There is less need for quantity when the qualities of what you have can keep you awestruck.

Love as Looking Deeply

In the book *The Lime Twig*, John Hawkes says, "Love is a long, close scrutiny." Love is a matter of languid time and curious engagement. Know that the more deeply you offer your interested regard to someone, the more likely it is that love will emerge. To look closely is the opposite of taking something for granted. Choose someone every day and take more time than usual to offer them your interest and attention. One extra question can change an ordinary exchange into an extraordinary connection. One expression of appreciation each day can transform an existing relationship into one you have dreamt about.

✳

What ordinary things can you pause right now to see as
extraordinary?

✳

To whom can you offer heartfelt appreciation today?
How will you show it?

EYES INTO THE WORLD

For someone who relishes long, summery days of sunlight, early winter in New England can be hard. At first glance the view is ordinary — monochromatic grays and browns. But intentionally refocusing my gaze and looking more alertly, I see abundant beauty calling out for my notice. I perceive shades of every color — in the lichen on the bark, the gnarled apples still hanging on a tree, the amber of a lone beech with its leaves still quaking. I know that the best of life and love asks for my "long, close scrutiny." I know rigorous curiosity as the only way to experience the nuances of splendor and the subtleties of love. But I often forget to remember. Beholding makes the difference between saying someone has brown eyes, and letting our gaze reveal that colorful flecks of lichen, apples, and beech all live in those brown eyes, too. It opens my heart and my senses to notice more. I need to remind myself again and again that slowing down to notice beauty and blessings delivers all the riches I have been longing for.

4. APPRECIATION IS GENERATIVE

I would rather be able to appreciate things I cannot have than to have things I am not able to appreciate. — Elbert Hubbard

Appreciation brings about a shift from passively to actively engaging with life. We recognize that we have choices when it comes to orienting our attention. We see that we can notice and respond to the opportunities we have in each moment — not only our circumstances — and it shapes everything. Awareness makes it possible to become active practitioners in shaping our experience. Focusing on noticing and nurturing what we appreciate is a matter of agency. Doing this in all the ways that we can, whenever we can, is an important aspect of grateful living.

Poet David Whyte says, "Being unappreciative might mean we are simply not paying attention." But where should we focus our attention? Grateful living invites us to concentrate on what we already appreciate, and what we wish to appreciate more. It gives us the opportunity to appreciate things we never appreciated before. Appreciate is an active verb and calls for active engagement.

What we celebrate with our attention will grow and thrive. Appreciation turns strangers into friends, food into a feast, creativity into art, and people into their best selves. Appreciation can turn our planet into a sacred home and our communty into an extended family. These shifts in consciousness can deliver needed change to our world. The recognition and acknowledgment of worth can go a long way in uplifting and empowering others, our values, and the future we envision.

Tend What You Value

If you actively tend anything, it is likely to flourish. Tend a houseplant, a pet, a room in your home, or one of your core values, and you will see a response. Tend the streets around where you live by picking up litter. Tend your community by getting involved. Tend the well-being of a local business by choosing to be a regular customer. Tending a person is a most powerful appreciation practice. In Dr. Edward Tronick's well-known Still Face Experiment, simply offering or depriving infants of a smile had a profound impact on their emotional well-being and resilience. We are all built to be responsive to affection and attention.

This principle asks that what we say we value is actually reflected in our choices and actions. It is easy to espouse values and to speak of appreciation, but it is a whole other practice to invest ourselves in the things that matter to us. Walking the talk. Practicing what we preach. These are barometers for integrity. What we appreciate most in life should be obvious to an onlooker. Grateful living challenges us to align our actions with our values.

What You Value Thrives

There are so many opportunities in a day to tend the things that we value, and to bring them more alive in our attention. The nourishment that we can give to the things and people we care about is virtually endless when we actively appreciate them. Investment matters. Care wants to be shown. And in the process of tending what we love, *we* are enlivened. In appreciating others, we feel more interconnection and belonging. Tending the Earth reminds us that we are in this together and that everything we do matters and makes a difference. Celebrating what we already have is an act of cherishing and helps us feel content and replete. Given our inherent belonging, the more we share our appreciation for the gifts of life, the more everything around us thrives, and so do we.

PRACTICES
Appreciative Attention

Commit to tending one thing you may have neglected. Start with something that was a treasured item when you first got it: a houseplant, a piece of furniture, artwork, clothing, a keepsake, or a photograph. Make a practice of actively appreciating it every day to bring it back to its original appreciation-worthy state. It might need deep cleaning, organization, repair, or spiffing up. Once you have given it all the attention it needs, consider giving it away to someone who might appreciate it even more than you. With the practice complete, choose another item.

Gift Them with Kindness

It takes so little to make someone's day. When someone offers you a service — waiting on you at a restaurant, standing behind the register at the grocery store, helping you on the phone — shower them with kindness. It costs nothing to be generous with praise, appreciation, patience, and respect. Simply saying "Take your time" is enough to make someone feel seen and respected. Try saying this, even if you are in a bit of a hurry. Notice the response. Be free with your acknowledgment. It may truly make someone's day, and it may make yours as well.

Values Engagement

Find an organization doing work that advances your values. The focus could be education, healthcare, civic engagement, social change, civil rights, environmental advocacy, or some other worthy cause. There are many ways to show your support — donating money and volunteering time are only two. Consider bringing your creativity or outreach skills to the table. Attend events, write thank-you notes. The most useful path is to inquire as to what is needed, and then respond accordingly. These kinds of small daily investments multiply our efforts and effectiveness in helping to shape a thriving world.

*

Where is your appreciation most needed right now?

*

What do you care about that you want to help thrive?

INTENTIONS OF ATTENTION

There is a quote I have had on a Post-it note above my desk for years: "It is amazing how long it takes to complete something you are not working on." These words have resonated so intensely with me that I have carried this little reminder with me through many an office move. The note might as well say, "It is amazing how long it takes for someone to know you love them if you are not loving them." Or, "It is amazing how long it takes for something to flourish if you are not nourishing it." It speaks of alignment between intention and action, between actually tending to something that matters to you or getting off the proverbial pot. It is a call to my heart to remember what it values and to make that commitment and care evident in my moment-to-moment choices. It is a call to integrity. I did not know it when I first wrote myself that reminder, but it is a call to the practice of grateful living.

5. LOVE IS TRANSFORMATIVE

What gives me hope is that life unfailingly responds to the advances of love. — Nipun Mehta

Love is our nature — essential to us and essential to life. Love lives deeply rooted within each of us, protected from the comings and goings of people and circumstances. It simply exists as a force within us and around us. Love wants to come alive, and does so through a variety of expressions: poetry, music, touch, prayer, cooking, art, caretaking, work, kindness, service, gratitude, and more. Whenever we nurture and tend the things we value, that is love in action.

Grateful living is a practice of love in action. When our hearts are awakened to love, our availability to life and our capacity to cherish it increase. Compassion is naturally activated in the corners of our hearts when we are lit up by love. We see each other and the Earth as kin, as interconnected for good. A loving and grateful heart is a generous heart. All of the goodness that love delivers will find grateful reception in everything and everyone interested in waking up. What a blessing that our love can be awakened, offered, and received.

Embrace the Great Fullness of Life

The greater our capacity to be with the messy and painful parts of life, the greater our capacity to experience love. They flow into and from the same vulnerable heart. If we try to control our experience of life and love, we close ourselves off to the unexpected and surprising gifts of grace and belonging. Love is resilient enough to remind us of itself, even in painful times. This trustworthy love can acknowledge the presence of beauty in the midst of despair and struggle. Love that acknowledges the fullness of our truths delivers courage. It is an activator. When we open our eyes wide, our hearts follow. When we open our hearts, our actions follow. Love that stands to face the "full catastrophe," as Jon Kabat-Zinn calls it, is tenacious and fierce, capable of deeply touching and transforming lives.

Your Heart Overflows

Grateful living fills your heart to overflowing. In making yourself more conscious of and connected to the beauty, wonder, and opportunities of life and the people who surround you, you are able to be filled up. When love flows from this experience of fullness, it spills over into acts of kindness and compassion. It cannot help itself. This kind of love flows in an ever-replenishing cycle.

PRACTICES
Uplift Belonging
Love can emerge from our sense of connectedness and essential belonging. You have a seat at the table of life. You are a chosen, esteemed guest. As life delivers opportunities to gain perspective and you can see yourself as essential in the big picture of life, love emerges from a feeling of interconnectedness. Imagine sitting at a table so long that it stretches as far as the eye can see in both directions. The chairs are filled with a diverse array of humans and other creatures who belong here with you. Feel your heart warm and a smile come to your lips with a sense of family as each person raises a glass to toast our shared belonging.

Radical Hospitality
Radical hospitality means honoring the truth of all that we cannot anticipate and control, and all that arrives unexpected or uninvited. Commit to leave nothing out, including mystery. Greeted with open arms and an open heart, every part of life can find its place at the table. Hello, heartbreak. Welcome, joy. Come on in tenderness, doubt, vulnerability. Fully welcomed and held with compassionate love, these guests are more likely to come and go in a way that serves life.

Great Fullness Overflowing
Cultivate a compassion practice for the great fullness of your life and let it ripple out to others. Whenever you feel depleted or overwhelmed, say to yourself, "My great, full heart overflows with compassion." Inhale slowly with "My great, full heart," and then exhale on "overflows with compassion." Feel the soothing rhythm as you direct this compassion to yourself, and then imagine it going toward known and unknown people who might need such grace. Let this practice fill and refill the wellspring of your heart.

✴

How can you make the home of your heart more unconditionally hospitable?

✴

Where does the great fullness of your loving heart want to overflow — and in service of what?

A FULL HOUSE OF FEELING

Joy and grief live in the same house in my heart these days. When one emerges, the other usually tags along. They both want to be loved, often at the same time. Love needs to hold a very big open house in my heart. All my many feelings want acceptance and acknowledgment. When I cut one of my feelings off, it can get needy or rowdy. Feelings are attention-seekers and will knock louder if they think the door is closed. I often need to pause to give them their due dose of love. When they are satisfied I can carry on whatever I was doing. Sometimes they take me on journeys. The home of my heart is burgeoning these days: Joy. Fear. Grief. Love. Doubt. Vulnerability. Sadness. Grateful living has made them quite a harmonious community. The blessing that love offers is a graciousness toward all these same feeling states in other people. My home keeps growing as my doors open wider. There are plenty of seats at the table.

PUTTING PRINCIPLES INTO PRACTICE

Grateful living is a way of life grounded in meaningful principles that will help you to wake up and appreciate the life you have. The central grateful living practice of *Stop. Look. Go.* is simple yet surprisingly profound, and will leave you with greater presence, perspective, and possibility to bring to every moment.

The Five Guiding Principles

Life Is a Gift.
When you greet each moment gratefully,
you are always receiving.

Everything Is Surprise.
When you open to wonder, opportunities abound.

The Ordinary Is Extraordinary.
When you take nothing for granted,
life is abundant.

Appreciation Is Generative.
When you tend what you value,
what you value thrives.

Love Is Transformative.
When you embrace the great fullness of life,
your heart overflows.

CHAPTER 3

THE PRACTICE OF GRATEFUL LIVING

Stop. Look. Go.

By focusing on that for which we are grateful, by practicing gratitude every single day, by seeking out the beauty and positivity in every waking moment, we can create our very own ... abundance.
BROTHER DAVID STEINDL-RAST

✳

To be present to your life as it unfolds, to occupy each moment with a grateful heart, and to notice with curiosity what is happening inside and around you — all this delivers the possibility of contentment and joy. And all of it is facilitated by practice. It may seem odd that you would need to "practice" being available to life, but where we offer our attention, and how, shapes the ways we live our moments, and therefore how we experience our lives. Practice makes your moments more intentional and vivid. And it allows you to be more available to what matters most to you in life.

You will notice that simply making a commitment to grateful living as a practice in and of itself sends vital messages to your cells, your mind, your heart, and those around you. These messages help remind you to savor the life you have and be more available for its gifts. Committing to living gratefully helps reveal all the reasons you have to be thankful — waking you up to things you may have never noticed before and many you may have taken for granted. It opens your senses wider, focuses your awareness more intently, and orients you toward appreciation.

Recognizing that we are always practicing something, we develop the capacity to become more mindful of opportunities, and to shift our awareness toward that which awakens and serves us. When we practice, we guide our hearts and focus our minds to more readily access gratitude for the gift of life — so precious and worthy of our care and humble celebration.

Many of us need to cultivate reliable methods and practices to connect with or reinvigorate grateful awareness when it is not readily accessible. *Cultivation* harnesses the energy of our intentions. Just as we can cultivate a bountiful flower or vegetable garden, so too can we cultivate qualities in our lives we desire and that will serve our lives. What we nourish with our attention will nourish us in turn.

Grateful living weaves greater awareness throughout all of our moments. Like other forms of practice, grateful living offers a way to approach, frame, and learn from everything that unfolds in our lives, allowing us to access deeper reserves of resilience and wisdom. When you commit to practicing something, you become its student. You become attuned to its presence and promise. The good news is that the path of practice is deeply merciful; there is no doing it wrong. There is only the gentle reminder and opportunity to return again and again to your intentions, perhaps just one more time today, or simply one delicious moment more than yesterday.

Brother David Steindl-Rast lays out this simple yet rich prescription for how to practice grateful living: *Stop. Look. Go.* Most of us know this maxim by heart from when we were children standing at the curb with an adult next to us. It helps us harness our awareness, open all our senses, pay close attention, note the opportunities, and only then act purposefully. When we set out to meet the moments in our lives as if we were crossing a street, we cultivate attention, intention, and action: we stop, we look, and then we go. Following this rule preserved our lives as kids, and as adults it can help preserve our availability to live gratefully.

Stop. Look. Go. focuses us on cultivating three characteristics essential for a grateful life: presence, perspective, and possibility. When we *stop*, we become more present. When we *look*, we seek the gifts of a grateful perspective. When we *go*, we awaken possibility.

✻

What are some current practices you have or use in your life?

✻

What are some qualities you seek to cultivate, and what are some ways you do this?

A PRACTICE IS PRACTICE

I have to admit to having meditation envy — the way some people have car envy or house envy. I look at people who maintain a regular, sitting meditation practice and I feel unabashedly covetous and often self-incriminating. I more often drink tea, putter in the kitchen, talk with a friend, wander outdoors to look at the garden, read poetry, or go for a walk. Even while writing every morning — undoubtedly a practice — I can feel like I am faking it as a practitioner until I realize how grateful I have been whenever I was *not* thinking I should be sitting with my eyes closed on a meditation cushion. In those times of comparison, I try to remember to pause and notice how present I have been for whatever I was doing, how much perspective and sense of possibility I have gained because of it. Then I realize that I have actually been fully alive and grateful, and I remember why grateful living practice speaks so deeply and mercifully to my heart.

STOP: CULTIVATE PRESENCE

Gratitude is an essential part of being present. When you go deeply into the present, gratitude arises spontaneously. — Eckhart Tolle

We can be sure of this: our moments are passing. This moment greets us as wholly alive now, then it goes, and we have no idea how many more moments are ahead of us. This singular truth shapes all of our lives and levels the playing field for everyone.

You choose how to engage with the moments you have — this is your opportunity for creation. Time is your medium. You are the artist. How you choose to spend your time says more about you than just about anything. It defines each of us. Our choices become who we are, the life we have, and, ultimately, the life that we lived — our legacy. But we can easily feel more like victims of our time than artists. In this day and age, our moments seem to pass more quickly with everything moving at an accelerated pace. Living gratefully reminds us that there may be no way to fully catch up, but we can always *show up* more fully.

We live in a culture where our attention is a sought-after commodity and the feeling of insatiability fuels our economic engines. It can be hard to feel that this moment and our individual life are enough. We can gravitate toward a fixation on to-do lists, goals, aspirations, entertainment, consumption of various kinds, and anything to fill and "busy" the moment at hand. When our "now" is disconcerting, we perseverate about the past and worry about the future. A simple spaciousness of presence can be disarming in its quiet grace and invitations. But learning to embrace the expanse of the present moment is the only true way to live a conscious life.

It is a sacred act to pause. And it has become a radical act to stop, or even to slow down. Becoming more present to the moment is an intervention in automation. It wakes us up and keeps us from going through the motions or sleepwalking through life. It introduces the opportunity for consideration and contemplation, and the possibility of recalibration.

One of the reasons we might avoid pausing to be more present is that it opens us to vulnerability and everything that comes with it — messy and magical, tumultuous and tender, serious and sacred. But meeting the moment with presence is the gateway to perspective and possibility. Simply being available to all of "what is so" in any given moment is what opens our eyes and hearts to life. This can allow for deeper feelings of belonging as well as isolation, longing as well as satiation. Presence ushers in awareness of the preciousness of life as well as the certainty of its ending. Ironically, it is only through strengthening our capacity to be with vulnerability that we will become more at ease with being present. And vice versa. This is one meaningful purpose of practice.

When we are fully in the moment, we will be frequently surprised and able to learn from life as it unfolds. How can we possibly take things for granted when we behold the ever-renewing ever-newness to life? Slowing down allows us to notice the nuances of our feelings and experiences, and this is what makes insight possible. And insight can shift everything in favor of greater ease and wisdom. The biggest challenge is that our most painful thoughts often hijack our attention and convince us that to step out of their fray would be useless or a betrayal. When in truth, learning to quiet an actively tumultuous mind in favor of the sanctity of the present moment is one of the most useful and powerful things we can do for our well-being.

PRACTICE
Become Fully Present

Take a few minutes to focus on becoming fully present to the moment as it is. Use your breath and your senses to simply notice wherever and however you are. Even one conscious breath can deepen or shift your experience. Pause for greater presence as many times in the day as you can. It will generate innumerable gifts.

> Pausing for stillness, I am aware . . .
> Taking a deep breath, I notice . . .
> Tuning into my body, I feel . . .
> Embracing silence, I hear . . .

✳

What is a recent situation that would have benefited from your ability to take a breather and pause to cultivate greater presence?

✳

What is a recent experience in which you recall noticing the benefits of being fully present? What distinguished this moment from the one you reflected on in the previous question?

GIFTS OF PRESENCE

The practice of cultivating presence is most remarkable to me when I am busiest. When I am under a tight deadline or juggling more things than feels reasonable, I get to regularly notice how challenging it is to be fully in the moment with enjoyment. I tend to wish for more time so I can get more done, or I wish I was already done. Both wishes effectively obliterate the moment at hand. Time seems to fly by so much faster when it already feels tight. I find myself continually having to cultivate awareness of the present moment. I remind myself over and over that the opportunity to have so many things to which to attend is a privilege and a blessing. These reminders work. This is the practice in *practice*. Even while writing this, taking a deep breath, slowing down to notice all that is extraordinary about this very moment and opportunity, I feel much more fully here, tender, and grateful.

LOOK: CULTIVATE PERSPECTIVE

The tiniest change in perspective can transform a life. — Oprah Winfrey

When Brother David invites us to *Look* — after stopping for presence and before going toward possibility — he is directing us to seek the opportunity for enjoyment that awakens our grateful hearts. We are invited to look for the surprises that would bring us delight. We are to notice the things we take for granted, now seen with freshly appreciative eyes. The beauty we missed while sleepwalking through the day. The opportunity to be grateful that is knocking just beyond our ability to hear it in the tumult that surrounds us.

In many moments, simply looking for beauty, surprise, and opportunity can be enough to deliver enjoyment — and with it a grateful outlook. You can direct your attention or ask yourself a question, and something you can feel grateful for will appear in your field of vision or awareness. These are times in your life to be cherished — the times when it is relatively easy to be grateful.

PRACTICE
Look with Fresh Eyes
Take at least one minute to notice some of the opportunities to be grateful that are readily available to you right now. Consider these prompts:

Looking for reasons to be grateful, I notice . . .
Looking for beauty, I see . . .
Looking for surprise, I discover . . .
Looking for opportunities to be grateful, I am aware . . .

But there are many times in life when simply directing our gaze or attention is not enough to readily deliver gratitude. What is before us might not immediately speak to beauty, surprise, or opportunity — so we need to be able to see what is before us differently. One of the many gifts of perspective is that we can significantly change what we see by changing *how* we see. After a power outage, we shift from begrudging the clunky old lamp to celebrating the gift of its light. When we are truly hungry, we see the feast hiding in our vegetable drawer rather than just old produce. A loved one makes it home through a bad storm, and the morning's disagreement melts away. Perspective helps us add context and consideration, allowing us to see what's in front of us in a new way because it allows us to see with a wiser and more grateful heart.

You acquire perspective through experience and intention. It arises from what you choose to focus on, how you choose to see it, and the interior place from which you do the looking. We have influence over all of these. We can gain perspective by either moving closer or putting distance between ourselves and what we observe. It can allow us to be fully present to an experience and simultaneously be its witness. Perspective can let us put ourselves in someone else's shoes, a future moment in time, or the vantage point of a bird's eye view.

There are encounters that broaden our perspective and those that constrict it, attitudes that open up greater awareness and those that batten down our hatches, questions we ask ourselves that expand our consideration and those that limit it. Certain people and settings open us to perspective; others shut us down. The good news is that perspective enhancement is a practice that can be learned. Our work is to continually reset the aperture on our lens, inviting the focus and frame of reference that best allow gratefulness to surface and serve us.

We have all gained or lost perspective in the blink of an eye. We both consciously and unconsciously need to seek and re-seek it, sometimes hundreds of times a day. With grateful living, we can redirect our attention with prompts, short practices, questions, and reminders. We do not have to physically go somewhere for perspective (although travel is an exceptionally effective and enjoyable way to come by it). We can use memory or imagination to access other ways of seeing a situation. We can purposefully shift our thinking in ways that enhance our understanding of life.

Perspective is simply another way of experiencing the truth of what is. It is not an "attitude adjustment," because what we are experiencing isn't wrong. Instead, we gently layer on awareness, redirecting our attention to concurrent truths. Perspective helps us to remember that beauty and heartache coexist, as do grief and gratitude, joy and sadness. The dividends of perspective are reaped long term, arriving when our gratefulness accounts are near empty. Insight and wisdom come unexpectedly, but we need to sow their seeds all the time. We honor the longing to feel more grateful by honoring the wisdom of what is true. Learning to cultivate a more grateful perspective can make all the difference in how we experience most anything, and most everything.

✳

What activities or reminders help expand your perspective when it feels small, or help you find perspective when it feels lost?

✳

When your perspective feels enhanced, how do you experience your life and act differently?

WISE RESTLESSNESS

In the last four hours of writing, I have restlessly done at least ten different things to try to shift my perspective. I moved my laptop outdoors and then came back inside. I shifted to handwriting, then returned to the computer. I went to the kitchen to snack. I stood at my desk; I sat at my desk. I switched to a bigger monitor. I went back to the kitchen. In each of these moments, I really only saw myself as fidgety and unfocused. I was not aware of any of these acts as conscious attempts to enhance my perspective, but every single one was effective in some way that I can only now see. I keep learning: it is good to be curious and trust ourselves at the times when we think we are merely distracted. We are often wisely doing exactly what we need to gain a more expansive or informed outlook, but only if we let ourselves follow where we are guided. Intuition and impulse are often confused for each other. Being curious about my impulses as attempts to gain perspective keeps proving to be a good perspective to practice.

PRACTICE
Enhance Your Perspective

When your circumstances are challenging, looking for reasons or opportunities to feel grateful can leave you coming up empty. Use these reflection prompts and take some time to focus your attention on enhancing your perspective. Let yourself hold each of these prompts until it calls forth something meaningful from your heart.

Taking nothing for granted, . . .
Understanding that things could be worse, . . .
Seeing my life through others' eyes, . . .
Recognizing my relative good fortune . . .

Five Points of Perspective

As you begin to *Look*, there are Five Points of Perspective that will help you practice grateful living: embrace poignancy, invite peak awareness, acknowledge privilege and plenty, align with your principles, open to pleasure.

These points of perspective help you see things in new ways. Each one opens the aperture slightly differently, letting more light and information flood into what you can observe and sense is possible. In your daily life, you routinely enhance and shift your perspective, mostly without being aware. We are constantly making shifts in our attention so as to be more resilient and effective. It is valuable to become aware of the ways that perspective supports us to live gratefully, as it is of such profound benefit to our individual and relational lives.

Embrace Poignancy

As the last butterscotch sunbeams of summer light pass across the grass, you stand in awe, wanting to capture the radiance and hold it inside you.

Saying goodbye to someone you love dearly, you allow yourself to feel the weight of affection, vulnerability, and longing in your heart as you hold your hug longer than usual.

The nuanced meaning of poignancy has been lost in our common vernacular. When someone says something is poignant, we might think they are implying it is overly sad. But poignancy is actually a state of being deeply touched. It naturally accompanies our awareness of the limitation of time in the midst of meaningful experience. Poignancy heightens our senses and unleashes some of our most powerful emotions. It allows joy and grief to coexist harmoniously. You are holding a perspective of poignancy when:

- You feel mixed emotions. Grateful sadness. Sweet melancholy. Sorrowful joy. Heartbroken care. Deep, tender, vulnerable love.

- You are aware that the great fullness of life has everything in it — the tension of all things beautiful and difficult occurring simultaneously.

- Life feels precious, precarious, fragile, fleeting, meaningful, ephemeral, and moving all at once.

- Bittersweet recognition reveals that all blessings are for this moment, and a relief that this means most hardships are temporary as well.

Poignancy aligns perfectly with the first grateful living principle: *Life Is a Gift*. This principle helps you remember that when you greet each moment gratefully, you are always receiving. Poignancy is a rich and provocative invitation to embrace paradox: we know poignancy whenever we hold love in the same space as we hold awareness of impermanence. Poignancy cracks our hearts open and makes us want to treasure what is available for us to love now.

✳

*Aware that life is beautiful and fragile, I am awakened
to what matters.*

✳

I greet each passing moment as precious.

✳

How would embracing poignancy offer you a
more grateful perspective?

Invite Peak Awareness

Surrounded by people — known or unknown — you feel suddenly overwhelmed and moved by the shared vulnerability of being human. You stand transfixed in awe at our common ground.

Standing at the edge of a body of water or mountaintop, the vastness of the world cracks you open to the oneness of all life and you sense your true belonging.

Peak experiences are those that engulf all our senses and leave us feeling more connected than ever to ourselves and our shared humanity. These experiences can also deliver us into awe and a larger landscape for hope. *Peak awareness* refers to the insights gleaned from our moments of peak experience. You are holding a peak awareness perspective when:

- You feel dwarfed by the vastness and breadth of life on Earth, and sense your relative stature in the solar system.

- You see yourself as an essential part of one shared, cosmic universe connected to what is true and spiritually abiding.

- You recognize the long arc of history behind you with all of its pain and courage — yours and that of humanity — and you feel the future stretching before you, inviting trust.

- Your feeling of connection to the diverse human family reminds you that there is suffering, hardship, heroism, beauty, and love everywhere.

Peak awareness is closely aligned with the second grateful living principle: *Everything Is Surprise.* This perspective helps you remember that when you open to wonder, opportunities will abound. It reminds us of the grandeur and mysteries of time and space and that we are not in charge of everything. Peak awareness is often awakened by an experience of solitude in nature or in the midst of the hum of humanity, and it leaves us with an expanded vantage point. Like poignancy, peak awareness also holds paradox: in seeing life from 10,000 feet or with a view of the long arc of history, we feel our smallness. Peak awareness reframes our experience by reminding us that the eye of the beholder makes a difference — as does our vantage point.

✳

An expansive vantage point allows me to open to wonder.

✳

Seeing the big picture, I remember my inherent belonging.

✳

How do the insights of peak awareness offer you a more
grateful perspective?

Acknowledge Privilege and Plenty

Everything that works about your body, your mind, and your life, and all the ways in which you are not struggling suddenly strikes you as a great gift and you feel blessed.

The feeling of being safe and comfortable in your home, reaching for what you need and finding it there, awakens a sense of deep thankfulness.

Making a practice of regularly acknowledging all that is sufficient and plentiful in our lives allows us to access an experience of privilege, meaning an awareness of our relative good fortune. You are holding a perspective of plenty and privilege when:

- You recognize that many of your old wants and wishes have come true and you now have many of the things you used to dream about.

- You realize that all the ways in which your body works and is healthy would be the answer to many people's prayers.

- You are aware that most of the tangible blessings in your life have come from the generosity and efforts of countless people.

- You experience your comforts as luxuries, and everything that works as worthy of thanks.

Recognizing the plenty in our lives connects us to the third grateful living principle: *The Ordinary Is Extraordinary*. This helps you see that when you take nothing for granted, life is truly abundant. Affirming how we are not suffering or lacking in what we need and how much is accessible to us helps us recognize the blessing of having ease in many areas — ease to which not everyone has access. Privilege is a matter of perspective and encourages us to feel grateful and responsible. Ultimately, it will serve us to recognize the ways in which our lives are laced with plenty, and not only to know it but also to name it. To claim it. To share it. Because no matter who we are, we are surrounded and filled by things that make our lives extraordinary. Overlooking and denying what we have is to diminish our blessings and to disrespect their sources. Acknowledging the ways in which we are rich wakes us up to our windfalls, allows us to thrive, and helps our gifts flow to the benefit of the larger world.

✳

I notice all the ways that my life is working right now.

✳

My life is abundant in endless ways.

✳

How does acknowledging your privileges and plenty offer you a
grateful perspective?

Align with Your Principles

You connect with your innermost wellspring of values and beliefs and know without effort exactly what you stand for, and you stand taller inside.

Your sources of inner and outer guidance come into exquisite alignment, and you feel held and directed toward trusting yourself and life.

Our principles are present in the values and beliefs that orient us to life, offering guidance when we are seeking direction and reinforcement for our choices. Our overarching principles come from various sources in life, and the exact constellation is uniquely ours. You are holding a principles-informed perspective when:

- You tune in to yourself and feel that there is alignment between how you are choosing to live and what you believe to be most important.

- You seek to embody wisdom in making a difficult decision and you confidently look to your inner compass.

- You have the opportunity to take a stand for something you believe in and you can do so with fullness of heart.

- You turn to your principles for guidance and they do not fail you.

This perspective relates to the fourth grateful living principle: *Appreciation Is Generative,* and helps you remember that when you tend those things you value, what you value thrives. When we align with our principles, we align with the energy of our spiritual core. Possibility opens up — and we do, too. Our principles act like a spine keeping us upright in our actions, helping us to stand and to take a stand. When living gratefully, our principles allow us to access both internal and external wisdom from a place of being grounded in our beliefs.

✳

My integrity always offers trustworthy guidance.

✳

I am gratefully aligned with my values and beliefs.

✳

How does living in alignment with your principles support a more grateful perspective?

Open to Pleasure

Your senses are saturated by the beauty of a moment, and in order to soak in every bit of wonder and meaning so as to preserve it, you raise your arms to the sky.

You are so fully engulfed in gratitude for the enjoyment of an experience that you lose track of time and allow pleasure to fill you.

When we allow our senses to engage fully with life, we are available for the unexpected opportunities that arrive on the heels of wonder. We are alert for enjoyment. You can recognize a perspective of pleasure when:

- You open your senses to notice and channel creativity and play, and you find that they offer you unexpected insight and wisdom.

- You hold awareness of beauty and wonder as a paradox in the midst of painful moments, knowing that they, too, are true.

- You are awestruck in nature and experience resonance with yourself as an integral part of the natural world.

- You give yourself over with abandon to laughter and relax the tight grip with which you were holding life in your hands.

A perspective of pleasure connects us to the fifth grateful living principle: *Love Is Transformative.* This principle can help remind you that when you embrace the great fullness of life, your heart will overflow. We use our senses, savoring delights and tuning us in to creativity and the things that we loved when we were young. We are open to the presence of joy and the joy of presence. This vantage point supports us to behold people as if for the first or the last time, with reverence. A grateful perspective makes its home in all the possibility of love, and wants to be freely shared with others.

✳

I come alive when my senses celebrate beauty with abandon.

✳

Surrendering to love, I am connected with life.

✳

How can opening to pleasure offer you a more grateful perspective?

GO: CULTIVATE POSSIBILITY

This is not a time of mere change. This is a time of transformation, and transformation comes not out of scarcity but out of the context of possibility. — Lynne Twist

The final step in the *Stop. Look. Go.* practice is vital and differentiates grateful living practice from many other awareness practices. Doing something with the appreciation and opportunities that come our way brings the cultivation of presence and perspective into the service of our lives and life itself. This is how possibility comes to be. Grateful action is what puts the *life* into grateful *living*.

Living gratefully, we do not simply settle our bones when we can look around and pay homage to what we have in our lives that inspires our gratitude. Counting our blessings is a wonderful start, but the intention is to have the awareness of our blessings inspire us to live more wholeheartedly. The grateful heart wants to be expressed and shared; it wants to be lived. It recognizes our interconnectedness as its shared home and wants to benefit others. Once blessed with presence and perspective, gratefulness wants to cast its ripple, have its impact. *Go* beckons us to actively step into our lives and into the world, to finally engage with the possibilities waiting on the other side of the busy street.

Action that emanates from the grounding nature of presence and the guiding nature of perspective is necessary in difficult times. It is what will bring healing to the places that have been injured by misguided action. Acting from gratefulness when we feel moved is critical. Without presence and perspective, we often make messes — either in what is done or left undone, said or left unsaid. As the poet David Whyte says, "Regret is . . . an elegy to lost possibilities." Regrets stain our memories and make our hearts ache for what was misunderstood, unexpressed, or unfulfilled. To heal our regrets takes courage and an overflowing of the heart toward possibility. Preventing future regrets requires the same. With grateful living, we have the chance to wake up and devote ourselves to new possibilities, live from the fullness of our hearts, and suffer fewer regrets.

When opportunities knock, they rarely knock just once. They keep on arriving, and they all point us to possibility. Only when we are available to life can we hear and heed how we are called. Envisioning and investing in new possibilities is how transformation comes about. But how do we step into all the possibility that exists in a moment? We harness our big hearts and go forward with purposeful intention. We say "Yes!" to life.

✳

What motivates you to participate in shaping new possibility?

✳

How is possibility beckoning you — even quietly — right now?

THE POSSIBILITY OF POSSIBILITY

When I lose perspective, it is amazing how impossible things can feel, and how hard it is to be present. Then, when I get perspective again, everything seems possible. I often experience both these states in the same five minutes — okay, in the same minute. The line that divides them is very thin — it can be the subject line of an email, a lifeline that someone throws me when I feel like I am sinking, or a line in a book I am reading. In these moments, inevitably, a passageway opens to hope and imagination. Cultivating presence helps me feel grounded. Perspective helps me feel more grace, and more grateful. Regaining a sense of possibility flows readily from these states and can actually happen in short measure. But it is such a pleasure to pause for presence and perspective that I usually try to take my time. The practice of grateful living is an end in itself.

PRACTICE
Cultivate Possibility

Allow yourself to focus your attention on cultivating a sense of possibility. Notice what arises in you as you write or repeat the following prompts. Offer spaciousness for what wants to emerge, especially if a sense of hesitation comes up.

> My grateful heart moves me to act on behalf of . . .
> An opportunity clamoring to be chosen . . .
> Embracing my role in shaping what is possible . . .
> Where the great fullness of life meets the great fullness
> of my heart . . .

THE POWER OF *STOP. LOOK. GO.*

The transformative practice of *Stop. Look. Go.* will enrich your life. There is no aspect or moment of life that will not be served by becoming more awake and aware through presence. Presence allows you to be alert to the fullness of your life with greater wonder and opens you to perspective. Perspective expands your experience of life, allowing for greater appreciation of the opportunities available to you, and opens you to possibility. Possibility enlivens the moment at hand and animates your imagination and energy for what can be.

HOW TO LIVE GRATEFULLY MOMENT-TO-MOMENT

Grateful living is experienced and expressed in how you live the life you have. This life. Here and now. In the midst of any moment, if you simply pause to more fully notice and savor it before carrying on, this is grateful living in practice. This is *Stop. Look. Go.* as an everyday epiphany.

We live gratefully whenever we are awake, aware, alert, appreciative, and alive to our experience. Life delivers us opportunities in every moment: drinking tea, driving, making a meal, engaging in a conversation, going on a walk, sitting at your desk, taking care of someone, or brushing your teeth. There are as many ways to live gratefully as there are moments in the day. It can be elegantly simple. Begin wherever you are. Brother David says, "It is enough to be grateful for the next breath." Whenever you wonder how you might access gratefulness in a given moment, try this: Simply return to awareness of your breath — inhale and exhale gratefully. Recognize the fact of your aliveness. Tune in to your body as it breathes for you. Feel appreciation for the moment.

Invite your heart to soften into gratitude for the opportunity that life is offering you in this moment. Notice the ways that this is enough.

The practice of introducing simple moments and experiences of gratefulness into your day is profound. When you remind yourself of this practice throughout the day and string these moments together, you discover that these subtle internal shifts impact your sense of well-being. The commitment to living gratefully itself will yield tangible gifts and guide you, over time, to greater joy and peace. Trust this. And keep returning to your grateful intentions.

Be Creative with the Gifts at Hand

You can use the Five Guiding Principles as meaningful entry points whenever you need them. Say each of the principles aloud or to yourself, and become aware of their impact on you. Notice if you are drawn more to any one principle or part of one principle, and work with it as an intention, a mantra, or a daily reminder. Or use all five principles as a map to deepen your journey from one point of grateful awareness to another. You can also use the Five Points of Perspective in whatever ways work for you. Each point of perspective is accompanied by affirmations that can help guide you toward a grateful orientation. Explore their resonance and relevance in a variety of settings and circumstances.

Try bringing the guiding principles, points of perspective, affirmations, questions for reflection, and meditations from this book into your day in creative ways:

- Print them out on paper, cut them into strips, and put them in a bowl or basket where you can choose one every day as a focus.

- Let one of the statements guide your meditation practice for a time.

- Use one each day to say as grace before a meal. If you eat with others, let it catalyze a conversation.

- Use them as prompts for a morning writing practice, journaling, poetry, or a story. Or take photographs that capture their essence.

- Write them on sticky notes and post them on mirrors, your computer, the fridge, in a car, or other places where you will see them regularly.

- Share them with others in your email signature, add them to a business card, or make a greeting card from them.

- Try something creative. Paint them! Embroider them! Sing them! Write them with sidewalk chalk! Just use them to remind yourself and others that life is worthy of cherishing and celebrating, protecting and tending.

HAVE A GRATEFUL DAY

Life lays out a banquet of opportunities for you to engage in living gratefully. All the ingredients of grateful living are available to you, and each day is yours to make a bountiful feast. No matter what you do to remind yourself to take nothing for granted, how you arrive at openness for surprise, where you turn to notice beauty, or whom you choose to appreciate more fully — you are living gratefully.

Give yourself a grateful day that offers points of connection and practice:

- Rise in the morning with the Wake Up Grateful practice (page 27) — bring to mind three things you are grateful for before you get out of bed. Make yourself available to the gifts of your life from your first breath.

- Go through your morning rituals Doing It Differently (page 30) instead of by rote. Switch things up and notice how it wakes you up and brings a smile to your face. Be surprised by the blessings in your routines.

- While you are eating breakfast, focus on the Parts of the Whole (page 33) that went into making some of the things you use to prepare yourself a simple meal. Be amazed by our interdependence and connectedness.

- Whenever you drive, bike, take public transportation, or use a laptop, smartphone, or computer, think of how Well-Served (page 33) you are. Acknowledge your good fortune.

- When you interact with someone who is a regular part of your life, use the Love as Looking Deeply practice (page 34) and make sure they feel your care in specific, nurturing ways. Be generous with your interest.

- When you are out in the world and someone offers you a needed service, Gift Them with Kindness (page 36). Add praise and patience for an even better day. Leave a benevolent ripple.

- If you start to feel that you are going through the motions of doing your errands or chores, or if caretaking feels burdensome, use the Obligation to Opportunity practice (page 16). Feel the privileges of your full life.

- Take a little time to sit quietly, do the Insight-Full practice (page 27) to tune in to your intuition, and notice the guidance you are always receiving. Feel grateful for your own inner knowing.

- In the evening, go outside and look up at the sky for some Natural Inspiration (page 31) and gain a peak awareness perspective on life. Feel inspired and held within the vastness of our world.

- End your day with the Uplift Belonging practice (page 39). Notice how you can head toward bed connected to greater belonging. Nurture self-compassion and tenderness toward our shared human experience.

- Go to bed grateful. Put yourself to sleep with the Great Fullness Overflowing practice (page 39). Having done some of these grateful living practices throughout the day, allow yourself to feel the great fullness of your heart and sleep deeply, knowing that tomorrow is yet another opportunity to wake up grateful and take nothing in your extraordinary life for granted.

The Practice of Grateful Living

Stop.
Become Present.

Look.
Seek a Grateful Perspective.

Embrace poignancy.
Aware that life is beautiful and fragile,
I am awakened to what matters.
I greet each passing moment as precious.

Invite peak awareness.
An expansive vantage point allows me to
open to wonder. Seeing the big picture,
I remember my inherent belonging.

Acknowledge privilege and plenty.
I notice all the ways in which my life is working
right now. My life is abundant in endless ways.

Align with your principles.
My integrity always offers trustworthy guidance.
I am gratefully aligned with my values and beliefs.

Open to pleasure.
I come alive when my senses celebrate beauty
with abandon. Surrendering to love,
I am connected with life.

Go.
Awaken Possibility

PART II

GRATEFUL LIVING
IN THE
REAL WORLD

CHAPTER 4

SAVORING UNCERTAINTY

Diagnosis of Unknown Origin

It was a warm night in New York City, but not even a second down comforter could stop my whole body from shaking. Shivering chills and blazing heat had sent my internal thermostat climbing and falling like a roller coaster for days. By the third day of fevers over 102 degrees, it was time to get help. It was May 30, 1992. I was 32 years old.

I had moved to Manhattan for a job the year before and had friends nearby who drove me to a hospital in New Jersey. I was admitted for observation. I was observed, rigorously tested, and observed some more. But the fevers did not abate.

By mid-June, I was moved to a Manhattan hospital, where I was admitted with little more than "fevers of unknown origin," or FUO in diagnostic shorthand. This diagnosis was unusual in that it required me to remain an inpatient; it also made me particularly interesting to residents and physicians across a range of specialties. FUO is meant to be a temporary stop on the way to someplace more solid, someplace with a classification and protocols. Diagnosed but undiagnosed, I was presented at grand rounds and became the problem to solve, the case to crack.

Having a diagnosis that included the word *unknown* made me feel like my life had been reduced to one big paradox. FUO was something the doctors could scrawl on the clipboard hanging at the bottom of my bed and tuck into the folder outside my door. FUO gave me a private room and made my visitors don masks before entering. FUO satisfied the insurance company's need to justify weeks of hospitalization and expensive testing. And FUO allowed my employer to grant me an extended medical leave. But FUO answered nothing.

Unknown wedded me to uncertainty. To live inside a body about which I could offer no reassurance to my loved ones was confounding and painful. Their questions were an anxious and relentless chorus: What is wrong? What do you have? Why don't they know more? What are they doing for you? When can you get out?

We hung our hopes on every new possibility and I joined my doctors in promising everyone that the next test would provide an answer. Meanwhile, they questioned, tested, imaged, and biopsied. They attempted treatments for a variety of infectious diseases: malaria, tuberculosis, histoplasmosis. But the fevers came back while the misdiagnoses, negative tests, side effects, and ineffective treatment trials continued to mount. Increasingly, the only honest answer I was able to muster was, "They do not know. I do not know."

Every moment of not knowing was a source of suffering, often more so than the physical suffering of spiking fevers. I joined the medical professionals in being driven by the belief that just around the bend was the answer waiting to be discovered. If only we could determine the right test, we could finally find the solution. The promise of that end justified any and all means. I signed every consent form, agreeing to risks that I would have previously thought unimaginable — internal bleeding, paralysis, death. All in the hopes of knowing what was happening in my body and how to make it stop.

Everything changed with the mediastinoscopy — a last-ditch diagnostic intervention. The surgery for which the renowned specialist was on his summer sailing vacation in Switzerland, so we went with the available surgeon. The surgery after which the nurse told my family that I had almost bled to death. The one after which I developed a raging staph infection. The one in which they took out lymph tissue from around my heart that suggested cancer, but then the exact type of cancer fell into question. The pathology reports from four leading cancer institutions all came back with different results. Probable diagnosis: cancer. Exact diagnosis: inconclusive. Treatment plan: more diagnostic exploration.

Three months had passed and I was no wiser about what was wrong with me. I had no answer from doctors or the medical system. I did know, however, what I was experiencing, feeling, and coming to understand. I felt a strong desire to let go of pursuing a definitive answer. I felt a call to let go of an inherited, internalized belief that everything could be known, would be known, and should be known. The typical path of "if only we could get the right information from the right authority in the right way at the right moment, we would know something for sure," was not working. What I was coming to understand was that the physical and psychological costs, losses, and harms resulting from the quest for data were throwing the benefits out of balance. I suspected that I could be part of the solution by trusting my sense that perhaps we already knew enough, and that time would tell us more than any immediate diagnostic information.

Surrendering the drive for certainty was both terrifying and empowering. I learned to see hope as an unconditional orientation to life that called on me to bow to the one truth of which I had become certain: there is a mystery to life that is more vast and promising than what is knowable. And even though I had no idea what that mystery held, I knew it could hold me — and I was getting better at holding it. Within the embrace of all that was unknown and uncertain, I felt an unlimited aliveness well up in me that was greater than any aliveness the medical system was promising. In that spaciousness of my heart, I felt that every moment of my life mattered, and I wanted to live it — no matter what I knew or did not know, no matter how long I might or might not live.

HOLD SPACE FOR MYSTERY IN YOUR LIFE

Deep trust in life is not a feeling but a stance that you deliberately take.
It is the attitude we call courage. — Brother David Steindl-Rast

We all have wake-up calls that help us remember that life is precious and fleeting and we are not in charge. In the crucible of those moments, we are called to deepen our trust that the nature of life means perpetual uncertainty and that this uncertainty makes everything vibrate with possibility. We are called to remember that when we are truly present and open to life in its fullness, it is more expansive and inexplicable than any of us can imagine.

There are far more things we will not get to know than know. If this alarms you or makes you uncomfortable, can you reframe it as cause for wonder or surrender? There is much to discover, and so much to which we can yield when we let go. And yet when we experience uncertainty, it can be rattling. It goes against the conditioning most of us have internalized that "not-knowing" is threatening and must be overridden or resolved as quickly as possible.

Once we admit our tendency to want to forsake the unknown in exchange for reassurance and consistency, we can better make space for the riches of mystery. It helps to acknowledge the ways we are driven by the longing to reduce our lives to the tangible and predictable, and things about which we believe we can do something. We think we can control what we know. In the name of security and safety, we hold fast to the idea that with will and effort we can be in charge of our experiences, and often the experiences of others as well. We attach ourselves to lifestyles that assure desired outcomes for health, love, longevity, and success. And we turn to authorities and prognosticators — meteorologists, nutritionists, astrologists, psychologists, oncologists — to help us know what we might expect from life, and their prescribed path to get there. Even though they often prove themselves incorrect, and we experience the crush of disappointment time and again, we lean away from the promises of mystery, yearning instead for the promises of the predictable and expected.

All the while the great fullness of life with all of its unanswerable questions, unexpected opportunities, and startling surprises carries on, inviting us to embrace not knowing, and slide into the river of greater release and trust.

When you practice grateful living, you create a welcoming space for uncertainty, knowing that it arrives naturally in those moments when you take nothing for granted. Without expectations, life is one surprising unfold-ing after another. The exact nature of the surprises is not up to us, but our response is ours and ours alone. Each time we let go instead of holding on, we receive reinforcement for our willingness to surrender to mystery rather than resist it. We can turn our controlling impulses over to the larger designs of the universe, choosing to let go of our white-knuckled grip on the steering wheel. The rewards of this shift are ever available and make the risks ever worth-while, as they deliver greater well-being, resilience, and joy.

BECOME PRESENT TO MYSTERY

It's that knife-edge of uncertainty where we come alive to our truest power.
— Joanna Macy

Many of us have negative ideas about uncertainty — as the absence of ease, comfort, or clarity. Trying to relate to uncertainty is difficult because it is like trying to relate to a lack of something, not a presence. But coming into com-munion with absence is important. It can help to think of uncertainty as mys-tery, and mystery as having a palpable presence.

Mystery asks us to muster courage for the encounter. We can access deep reservoirs of trust each time we face that which beckons, and perhaps fright-ens, us just beyond the edge of our knowing, beyond the edges of our control. Every time we look into the depths of the darkness and live to tell the tale, we are nourished in our trust and faith. This is how we build our spiritual muscu-lature and how gratefulness comes alive.

Choosing to become present to mystery creates intimacy with those aspects of ourselves and life that do not always get the reverence they deserve. When we can hold our not-knowing with tenderness and curiosity, we develop comfort with our stillness, and vastness. Sometimes, simply exploring and affirming how intimate we already are with various forms of mystery can liberate us from feelings of fear and the need to control life. We then become able to receive — from within and around us — forms of wisdom and guid-ance that wait until the mind surrenders its need for certainty before the quiet beauty of possibility reveals itself to us.

*

When you are facing something uncertain in life,
what words or actions help you stay present and persevere
in the face of not-knowing?

*

How could you deepen your relationship to "the mystery"?

VOICES OF GRATEFUL LIVING

Even as I go through some difficult spiritual struggles, I can change my perspective by remembering that it is through my questions, doubts, and fears
that I will come into a space of deeper awareness and appreciation for the
mysteries and spiritual realities in life that encompass all of reality. It will
also allow me to offer others insights when they struggle on their spiritual
journeys. — Matt V.

SEEK A PERSPECTIVE OF SURRENDER AND TRUST

You are the sky. Everything else is just the weather. — Pema Chödrön

We hold — and are held in — mystery. The more we can create a grateful relationship to this fact, the better off we will be when life delivers itself to us in its
inestimable fullness. If we can, as Pema Chödrön says, see ourselves as the sky,
then unpredictable weather can pass without compromising our perspective.
We know we are bigger than the passing storm. We are vast enough to hold
our experiences, and the universe is vast enough to hold us. Weather comes
and goes. We need not define ourselves through it. We do not control it, nor do
we need to feel perpetually at its whim.

Responding like a victim to life's unfolding, at odds with its mysteries, can
lead us to develop vigilance. Vigilance can become our default setting for coping with the unknown, convincing us that if we are on alert, with our senses at
peak arousal, we can anticipate and therefore better predict the future. Vigilant
people stay tuned to the weather channel, radar, apps, and radio, imagining
that they can manage the upcoming storm — rather than seeing themselves as
the sky. Vigilance takes us out of the organic moment-to-moment arrival of life

in exchange for the illusion of control. And it is exhausting, as anyone who has lived in a state of consistent vigilance knows.

Almost everything you now know used to be unknown to you. And there are still plenty of unknowns that will make themselves known, and you will then be able to look back on any current uncertainty with a different perspective. When we let go of the idea that we can be in charge at all times, we develop more trust in the face of the unknowable. The more trust we extend, the more gratefully we can embrace not-knowing and learn from our experiences. We deepen our capacity to be with life as it is.

✳

In what areas of your life could you let go of vigilance, trusting that you can face and learn from whatever unfolds?

✳

When does perspective help you better surrender to the unknown and mysterious? What perspectives help?

AWAKEN POSSIBILITY IN UNCERTAINTY

The willingness to consider possibility requires a tolerance of uncertainty.
— Rachel Naomi Remen

Everyone who has ever lived — in their action and inaction — has shaped the world we occupy. The unknown future is the most inspiring invitation we can possibly hope for.

How different would it be if everything were already certain? If life's grand plan were 100 percent written without you or your forthcoming contributions folded into the story? Knowing that life is uncertain invites us to know that our actions matter and can make a difference. If there were no mystery, we could simply sit still and witness life unravel before our eyes like a movie. You would be a passive observer, excused from showing up for life. We could forgive ourselves our indifference because there would be no opportunity to make a difference. But life is no movie. The uncertain future awaits your particular presence, participation, and points of impact.

Cultivating curiosity for the unknown ahead — and courage for your yet unknown role in it — is paramount to living gratefully. You are the through line of your own story. You are the through line for the future. You are the constant that possibility is constantly awaiting.

To invest in the future while embracing the vast unknown is to hold a powerful paradox in our hands. Waking up to our lives exactly as they are, with appreciation for what we know and do not know — and making use of this opportunity to shape the best future for ourselves and the world — is our heart's calling. When we allow ourselves to remember and trust that there is nothing more we need to know in order to live fully, we will find ourselves more available to life, and life infinitely more available to us.

✳

What small actions can you take today that would embolden your sense of possibility for the future, even with all that remains uncertain?

✳

Who in your life is facing uncertainty with fear? How could you offer support to them from a place of compassion and courage, trusting in the mystery, befriending the unknown?

WE LOOK WITH UNCERTAINTY

We look with uncertainty
beyond the old choices
for clear-cut answers
to a softer, more permeable aliveness
which is every moment
at the brink of death;
for something new is being born in us
if we but let it.
We stand at a new doorway,
awaiting that which comes . . .
daring to be human creatures,
vulnerable to the beauty of existence.
Learning to love.
— Anne Hillman

VOICES OF GRATEFUL LIVING

Life is too full of awesome mystery and uncertainty for us to ever be able to fully understand and explain it. What a joy to be able to participate in this gift that can leave us ecstatic and smiling ear to ear and also in tears of heartbreak with questions that cannot be settled by simple answers. — Ian C.

GRATEFUL FOR EACH MOMENT

Hope locates itself in the premises that we don't know what will happen and that in the spaciousness of uncertainty is room to act. — Rebecca Solnit

While not knowing is not easy, it can also be a source of promise and freedom. It allows for all that is yet unknown to emerge and arise. These are the forces that invite the great fullness of life to become the furled pages of our histories. Goodness and hardship, both. The unknown allows for heartache, transgression, and illness, just as it makes possible love, healing, and sweet surprise.

Grateful living helps us focus on the creative possibilities before us and creating possibilities for more hope. Depending on how we approach and hold uncertainty, it can either enrich or constrict our lives. The invitation is toward gratefulness, supporting us to surrender our expectations, welcoming and trusting life as surprise. We begin with ourselves where we are, broadening our ability to partner with mystery in constructing lives worthy of meeting the uncertainties of the world with our whole hearts.

✳

*May you hold all that is unknown in this moment
with surrender and trust.*

Practices and Prompts

STOP. LOOK. GO. PRACTICE
Embrace the Gifts Inherent in Mystery
Though it has been said that "God is in the details," faith is something we can experience when we step back and allow ourselves to be dwarfed by awe. Tend to that sense of awe. Become aware of your place on a long continuum. Feel the

largeness of the global family and your small but pivotal place in it. You are a citizen of the cosmos. Feel connected in a vast network of time and space.

Now notice the many things you do in your day that have no guarantees. This not-knowing can occur in many different ways, on a spectrum from comforting to disconcerting. Strengthening your musculature to embrace mystery nourishes peace and gratefulness. Our sense of faith is nourished every time we take a risk or invest in something for which no particular result is promised, and yet we smile — inside and out.

Brother David calls faith "courageous trust." Where do you regularly live from courageous trust? How are you routinely investing in possibilities you cannot see, touch, or understand? When does finding peace require that you "let go to not know"?

> **Stop:** Relish the opportunity for slowing down. Become conscious of your breath. Follow one complete inhale-exhale cycle with close attention. Bring your awareness to the present moment and soften into it. No matter where you are, make an effort to tune in to the vastness around you. Picture yourself someplace where you can see far and wide, like a mountaintop. Fall in love with what you feel.

> **Look:** See your life from enough distance that it offers perspective and helps you feel the truth of the fact that, no matter what, we are united in not being in control of everything that happens.

> **Go:** Do something that takes courageous trust, and watch your "musculature for mystery" become more robust.

> - Commit an anonymous act of kindness or service. Expect nothing back. Truly. Smile inside. Do it more often.
>
> - Do something you have been afraid to do, safely. Survive it. Feel trust multiplying.
>
> - Plant seeds. Water them regularly, just a bit. Give them warmth and light. Be amazed.
>
> - Get yourself somewhere where you feel small. Feel how faith gets bigger when we can let go of needing to be big. Feel your own dawning.

Finding Mystery

Sit comfortably and take time to notice your breath. Allow your next exhale to take you into a place of peace with simply being present in your body. Right now you do not need to know, predict, or guarantee anything. Shift your intention to notice the presence of mystery. Take whatever time you need to settle into the awareness. Notice if images, sensations, or feelings arise. Does mystery have an essence or image for you? If so, invite yourself to feel its shape, its heft, its promise. Everything surprisingly wonderful in your life beyond this moment is held in this place. What holds mystery? How does mystery hold you? Sit for a few minutes and let yourself ponder the presence of mystery, and your presence with it.

Savor the Spirit of Uncertainty

Emily Dickinson writes: "In this short Life that only lasts an hour / How much — how little — is within our power."

Think about how much and how little is within our power in our short lives. How does this idea open possibility for you? How does knowing that we have a relatively short time on this Earth free you to live more fully into any and all uncertainty? What does this make you want to do? Try to act on this freedom in some way today.

PERSPECTIVE PROMPTS
Find Poignancy in Uncertainty

Once we believe that we know something, we tend to take it for granted and put it out of our conscious consideration. When this happens, the pulsing energy of uncertainty is gone. This is a true loss, as there is an exquisite poignancy in uncertainty. We can choose to love the questions we hold in our hearts and let them speak to us of things that matter and want our attention. We can magnify our curiosity for the wisdom of our future selves, and delight in being exactly where we are now, pulsing with a life-force for learning.

Without trying to override the places of not-knowing in your life, explore seeking the perspective you need directly from the moment and the heart of what is uncertain.

✴

*Life's mysteries are a gift allowing me the opportunity
to savor my questions.*

See Yourself as Part of the Human Family

With peak awareness, we know that throughout history and all over the
world, every challenging decision, every baby born, and every death has felt
uncharted to those in the middle of it. Every morning welcomed, every night
that has brought sleep, every journey undertaken — all of it exists against a
backdrop of uncertainty. To live and love in the face of all that we cannot know
takes courage. To think of ourselves as part of a human family across generations that has bravely faced doubt is to know the comfort of kinship.

Imagine yourself surrounded by the spirits of people of every background
and every generation who have lived with uncertainty like yours — and far
greater — and exhale into that belonging.

✴

Uncertainty connects me to the surprising realities of being human.

The Privilege of Certainty

Spend a minute focusing on some of the things you know for sure. Tried and
true formulas. Facts that hold up under scrutiny. We can search and confirm
or disprove things as we never have before in history. Technology offers us
answers to longstanding questions in seconds. We can learn words in a new
language with the help of our phones. How wonderful to have the privilege of
certainty. And what a welcome, gracious privilege uncertainty can be, too.

Consider the places of uncertainty in your life as spacious pockets of
respite from the work of knowing and having to know. Allow yourself to sink
into the mysteries of life with appreciation.

✴

*I am grateful for all that I am able to to know, and the privilege of
mystery that remains.*

Know Your Intentions

The Serenity Prayer was adopted into 12-step programs around the world in 1941: "God, grant me the serenity to accept the things I cannot change, the courage to change the things I can, and the wisdom to know the difference." It aims to deliver perspective when we experience fear in the face of what we cannot know or control.

The Serenity Prayer is a reminder that we can cultivate tranquility through surrender and rise to the challenging occasions of life through accessing courage. This kind of wisdom serves us in the many circumstances of not-knowing that we encounter every day. Many prayers and mantras help us align our spiritual commitments and approach to life with our intentions.

When a wave of uncertainty arrives, greet it with graciousness and equanimity, knowing that courage and wisdom wait for you in the wings, available when you need them.

＊

When I remember my intentions, they carry me with grace through uncertain times.

Find Pleasure in the Unknowable

Without the existence of all that is mysterious, we would live only with what is known and knowable. Imagine how our lives would shrink if everything unfolded exactly as we expected. How terribly one-dimensional it would be to construct and control everything. Instead, we have mystery to thank for the greatest joys and blessings in our lives: its unexpected teachings, the lessons that choose us, the love from across the room, the new friends, the chance encounters with beauty and inspiration, the gift of another day.

Think of times when beauty, love, and joy have surprised you. Know that their shared home is uncertainty.

＊

I welcome the many surprises uncertainty has in store for me, including love.

CHAPTER 5

TREASURING THE BODY AS IT IS

On Woundedness and Wonder

Having a body had been a relatively reliable source of delight and ease for most of my young life. Certainly, I developed the customary teenage body-image blues, and more times than I can remember, my knees got scraped, my ankles sprained, and my heart badly broken. But I always felt lucky that nothing significant had befallen me physically. No major bone breaks. No big surgeries. No hospitalizations. No serious illnesses. Just me and my body navigating life together, taking it all for granted — until I no longer could.

On a steamy August afternoon, after ten weeks of inpatient living, I finally left my New York City hospital for familiar environs, friends, and family in western Massachusetts. I had with me a plethora of gifts and get-well cards, a topography of new scars, and an inconclusive diagnosis of Hodgkin's lymphoma.

As unimaginable as it now seems, I spent the next months in diagnostic limbo — again. Under the care of doctors at a local hospital, many things got called into question — again. More conflicting pathology reports, inconclusive biopsies, aberrant test results, differing opinions, and the development of new, confounding symptoms. I was informed that the treatment protocols for different diseases and types of cancer were high risk and at odds with each other, and that there would be deleterious results if wrongly administered. Uncertainty was not letting go without a fight.

That winter, I succumbed to increasingly intense back pain. We initially thought it was from the immense amount of time I was spending in bed. But as the pain worsened and the drugs required to keep me comfortable were exhausted, it became dire. I remember lying in bed in a haze, being asked to rate my pain level. I thought of those charts in doctor's offices with faces numbered from 1 to 10. I wondered if there was a "12." I had never known such pain existed, and it was hard to imagine I would survive it. I wondered how other people did. I meditated on women the world over who had given birth. It helped.

In early March, after half a dozen vertebral biopsies with indefinite results, and the day after my thirty-third birthday, I underwent a successful lumbar resection and fusion surgery at Massachusetts General Hospital to remove my cancerous L3 vertebra. Rods were screwed in place to stabilize and "cage" the majority of my lumbar spine, something I was told would keep me from spending the rest of my life in a wheelchair. Renowned orthopedic surgeon Henry Mankin woke me to tell me that I indeed had Hodgkin's lymphoma that had spread to my spine — now stage IV — but that I was going to be okay, and one day I would come back to the hospital in an orange dress to dance the tango with him. I eked out, "Okay." What else could I say to an invitation like that?

For a month afterward, there were a precious few days when I was able to leave the confines of my apartment and move my new body slowly around town. Invariably, an acquaintance would stop me to tell me how good I looked. It was always shocking to hear, but I could imagine how it might appear this way to the eyes of the unknowing. Months of pain and surgeries had thinned my body from Rubenesque to one that fit better within the narrow confines of "normal" on the ideal weight charts. Weight loss of this magnitude seems to warrant excitement, praise, and envy. My thinness triggered people's ingrained assumptions about how well things must be going, and how happy and healthy I must be. It was truly an out-of-body experience each time someone remarked on how good I looked, when I felt like I was cheating death every day. I became more aware of the baggage we all carry concerning our bodies — and the gap that exists between what we assume when we look at another person, and what is true.

My illness taught me greater empathy for the wounded places inside everyone that we cannot see, touch, or imagine — and not to take what we see of each other at face value. So many of our illnesses, struggles, and disabilities are hidden, and many people who appear to have disabilities are, in other ways, far more intact than we might be. The most important parts of us long for the sincere invitation to show themselves and be acknowledged, in both our brokenness and beauty.

The surgery to remove cancer that had metastasized to my spine repaired me and readied me for treatment. But it did far more than that. It cracked me open, and taught me unmitigated awe for the capacities of the body to function, to repair and recover, to heal, and to carry on. It opened my eyes and heart to better appreciate the courage with which so many people live their days. The human capacity for tenacity and resilience is perpetually astonishing. I learned that our bodies are a never-ending blessing worthy of our full-blown, moment-to-moment appreciation and wonder — no matter what.

BEHOLD YOUR EXTRAORDINARY BODY

Our eyes see, but only our hearts look through things to find their meaning . . . Our ears hear, but only a listening heart understands.
— Brother David Steindl-Rast

Our bodies are a miraculous, mysterious landscape. Though you may tend to think of your "body" as merely what you behold in a full-length mirror, or as the parts that clamor and creak for your attention, your body is actually far more than what you see and feel, and far more than even the inner workings of your formidable, yet fragile, frame.

In this very moment, you are fully alive. Your body is quietly executing thousands of extraordinary feats simultaneously, mostly without your noticing, offering myriad blessings in every moment, mostly unconditionally. This fact alone should render us speechless. If all we ever did to inspire gratitude was to turn our attention toward how much is effectively happening in our bodies without our effort, we would find ourselves in a state of perpetual awe.

The simple practice of not taking your body for granted can open a door to great appreciation for life. It is difficult to turn our focus away from physical changes or distress, all of which seem to want every last morsel of our attention. But it is important to be able to directly experience the fact that with a slight shift in focus, the challenging sensations and experiences of the body are dwarfed by the larger context of all that is working. Learning to facilitate this shift in attention can have seismic ripple effects in many areas of our lives.

The body is paradoxical in all of its magic and messiness; it embodies us as it confounds us. It is both mighty and meek, independent and dependent, resilient and fragile. We can experience debilitating injury or illness in one part of us and absolute well-being in the rest. One day, we are healthy; the next, we are sick or impaired. We may wrestle with acute or chronic illnesses, addiction, or pain, and still appear absolutely physically fine to the outside world. Those who look unhealthy may outlive us by decades. Giving birth to new life: ecstasy and agony. Injury and illness: what was broken often heals with greater strength. Aging: as we experience diminishing physical strength and fewer days in which to take it all in, we simultaneously grow wiser and more comfortable in our skin.

Holding empathy for ourselves, we can lean into all of our bodily experiences with interest and curiosity, better able to welcome the lessons that are ours to learn, and ones that open us to even more appreciation. When we feel more connected to the body and its endless aptitudes, it is natural to want to comfort and care for it. Facilitating this empathetic connection with our bodies can deliver meaningful healing, and it is not necessary to wait until we feel more well, whole, or worthy to begin.

When you practice grateful living and hold your body as sacred, it leads to a gentler and more interconnected sense of wholeness and belonging. It is easier to remember that we all have bodies that require nourishment, experience pain and pleasure, generate comfort and discomfort, and accomplish great feats simply to function. You can become better attuned to the nuanced wisdom of the body and all its senses as you listen. Awakening the body to greater self-appreciation is its own reward, for the body is what we wake up in every day. It is literally where we live.

BECOME PRESENT TO YOUR BODY

The deeper we live the life of our bodies, the deeper is the upwelling of love.
— Stanley Keleman

It is the body that gives us life, this life, and the ability to be alive to experience everything: this moment, this feeling, this hardship, this sensation, this love. As long as we are still breathing, our bodies carry everything we are, everything we undergo, and everything we will become. The body is our sacred home.

We can count on the fact that our bodies will offer marvels and beauty, and we can also count on the fact that they will offer abundant opportunities to be disappointed and challenged. This goes with the territory of all that is beyond our control. We take up residence in our bodies, but our bodies are residents in the larger world. We bump into things, and people bump into us, sometimes by mistake, sometimes on purpose — all of it leaving imprints. We carry visible and invisible scars and wounds: evidence that we are vulnerable to and interconnected with the systems outside of us. No *body* is exempt from being impacted by forces beyond its control. No *body* is separate from the cascade of its history. This truth humbles and unites us all, and calls on us to deepen the empathy we offer ourselves and everyone we encounter.

When we allow ourselves to tune in to the body, there will be an abundance of sensation and instruction to notice. The body offers us infinite opportunities to gain insight and act accordingly. And, at the exact moment we may be dealing with the challenges it presents us, it will also present countless reasons to be reverent and grateful. The body wants our grateful companionship.

Committing to slowing down and communing with our bodies offers an experience of intimacy. When we take the space and time to notice what arises in and from our bodies, we can be enlightened. We can discover and heal a great deal of hurt with attention and appreciation alone.

> **Sensation:** Your body has the capacity for tremendous, endless sensation. You can attach all kinds of stories and feelings to sensations, but it is powerful to greet them as they are and listen to what the body is conveying. Understanding your physical experience as sensation opens you up to a more pure encounter with yourself, leaving the judgments of your mind out of the picture and allowing healing to have a presence.

> **Emotion:** You experience your emotions in intensely somatic ways. When you want to understand more about your emotions, it can be productive to turn toward the body to learn more. Where do you experience a feeling? How does it arise and change? What is it telling you or asking from you?

> **Intuition:** Your body carries wisdom and intuition to guide you. We call these messages our "sixth sense" or "gut instinct." If you invite your body's intelligence to surface, you can more quickly and accurately register when something is true and when it is not, or when a situation is to your benefit or when it is not. Intuition is alive and wise in the face of life's uncertainties, and your body is a tuning fork for truth — if you listen.

Befriending the body helps us remember that, as Jon Kabat-Zinn says, "as long as you are breathing, there is more right with your body than wrong with it." What may make the biggest difference in how we experience our bodies — and therefore in how we experience life — is where and how we focus our attention in any given moment. When we slow down enough to absorb the nourishment of our attention, and bring grateful perspective to our bodies, we can practice remembering all that is operating in our favor. In this remembering, we are better able to access the gifts of grace, empathy, and awe.

＊

When you slow down, settle into stillness, and regard your body as your one true home, what sensations and feelings arise?

＊

What aspect of your body are you aware of feeling most grateful for in this moment?

VOICES OF GRATEFUL LIVING

I started grateful living four years ago and noticed I was happier and had better relationships with colleagues and family. This year I had a traumatic skiing accident. I truly thought I was going to die. When I stopped falling, I knew I had broken my leg badly, but I was so grateful to be alive that I never complained about my leg. Four months after my accident, I'm still not walking but I'm getting there — every time I get down about it, I turn it around by remembering that it could have been so much worse. I'm grateful to be here and have the opportunity to rehab my leg back to normal!
— Jennifer E.

SEEK A PERSPECTICE OF AWE AND EMPATHY

I stand in awe of my body. — Henry David Thoreau

Every minute of every day, we take so much about the body for granted as it humbly chugs along, breathing, metabolizing, pumping, and moving us from one point to another. The body is truly extraordinary — we can and do count on it for so much.

With the sheer number of things that can go wrong at any time, and the number of forces that have to function and cooperate for any of us to get out of bed every day — much less move from one spot to another and do what we do — being alive is nothing short of miraculous. I don't use *miraculous* here to mean lightning bolts from heaven or having your one, big wish granted. It is simply so miraculous to wake up to another day that this alone can enhance our perspective enough to live gratefully. There is no end to facts about the systems of our bodies that can deliver us into awe if we offer our attention: circulatory, respiratory, digestive, immune. Each crucial to our well-being. Each inextricable from the others, collaborating doggedly to keep us alive every single day.

No matter what may feel imperfect about us, as long as we are here, there are so many things functioning perfectly at all times. Pause and allow these statistics to enrich your perspective:

- Your heart beats 100,000 times each day without your conscious effort.

- You take 1,000 breaths per hour without even thinking about it.

- You blink 1,000 times per waking hour, mostly without noticing.

- Your body produces 2.5 million new red blood cells each second.

- Your brain uses 20 percent of your body's oxygen and caloric intake, even though it is only 2 percent of your body mass.

- Your blood vessels are 60,000 miles long and could circle our planet twice!

Even if we cannot immediately cure what ails us, we can cure our perspective by learning to be with and treasure the truly amazing nature of the body. This kind of gratitude and compassion can help to serve the changes or healing that we may wish for, too. We can gain great benefit from choosing to regularly and intentionally marvel at our body as nothing short of an absolute, unconditional miracle.

✳

What aspects of your body inspire your awe?

✳

What parts of your body want to be held with empathy?

AWAKEN A SENSE OF POSSIBILITY FOR THE BODY

And I said to my body, softly, "I want to be your friend." It took a
long breath. And replied, "I have been waiting my whole life for this."
— Nayyirah Waheed

The mind-body connection is one of the most powerful relationships we have. Our intentions, self-talk, beliefs, fears, and longings all have impact. Our cells are reacting, dying, and being born in every moment, allowing for the body to both suffer an illness and transform from it. This transformation is not brought about by the will to *correct* the disobedient body you have, nor is it based on judgment disguised as self-love. Rather, it is a transformation at the level of collaboration, cooperation, compassion, and care — all available to us at any time as healing.

Healing is not the same as curing. *Curing* implies putting something completely behind us. Out of sight, out of mind. Healing brings everything with it, with thanks for lessons learned. Whether a cure is accessible or not, we can always heal, and we can always be an agent of healing for others. Leaning in with compassion and appreciation, we can nurture our connection to our bodies as we would care for a beloved child. This is a healing we need not wait for — and it is one that can never be undone.

When we entertain a sense of possibility, we move forward from exactly where we are, and exactly who we are. We do not need to wait to be better, different, or perfectly anything. We open ourselves to dreams and visions of what can be, mindful of the ever-present array of opportunities. With practice we can focus our attention on all that is intact, all that serves us, and continually remind ourselves that we are fully alive right now — and that being alive is an extraordinary, unconditional gift.

＊

When you feel truly grateful for your body exactly as it is, what are
you helping to heal? What other forms of healing feel more possible
from this place of grateful self-care?

＊

How might appreciating your own body increase your empathy and
compassion for the struggles of others?

FROM "HYMN, WITH BIRDS AND CATS"
I will praise my body whose middle-aged belly
Protrudes and whose knees have grown knobby,
This foolish animal shape who guilelessly
Stared back at me from the full-length mirror
Of a doctor's office two days ago.
Because it is still rain- and sun-loving matter,
the same that splashed lake water as a child
And rolled like a colt in June grass.
And I am never more satisfied than when I am
Walking or pushing or lifting with it,
Loving even the ache that follows,
That assurance I am rooted with earth.
— Francine Marie Tolf

GRATEFUL FOR EACH MOMENT

A desire to kneel down sometimes pulses through my body, or rather
it is as if my body has been meant and made for the act of kneeling.
Sometimes, in moments of deep gratitude, kneeling down becomes an
overwhelming urge, head deeply bowed, hands before my face.
— Etty Hillesum

Your body will disappoint and delight, betray and bless, hurt and heal you. Through it all, you can be sure of one thing: your body will accompany you through every moment of your life. It will hold you and all of your experiences as long as you are here. It is your formidable and delicate home.

Grateful living reminds you that the body is worthy of your most grateful regard and is always available to receive your care. No matter how broken you might feel, remember that you are always whole. And you are always a source of awe, just as you are. It is a hugely generative practice to bring greater tenderness and empathy to the body — yours and others'.

✳

May you hold the miracle of your body with awe and empathy.

PRACTICE
I'm Not Great, but I'm Still Grateful

When you're not feeling well, your body can become your sole focus. You may be tempted to freely share your ills when people ask how you are doing. But constantly talking about what isn't working to the exclusion of those things that *are* working can reinforce a sense of being broken or alone.

When, instead, you acknowledge the full truth of how you are — holding wellness and illness, challenge and ease simultaneously — you send affirming messages to your body and mind. You also send a powerful message to the people around you, giving them permission to have and share the well-rounded truth of their own full experience. This dynamic practice sets the tone for "both/and" language and helps you direct your attention to where it best serves you.

The next time you find yourself ruminating on your impairments, remind yourself that you may not feel great in all parts of your body, but you are very much alive, most of your body is working beautifully, and you can still feel grateful.

When someone asks how you are doing, experiment with offering this response: "I am not feeling great, and I am still grateful." Or, "Not great, but grateful." Notice how this allows for more of everything to be true at once — you are not entirely one thing or another. Notice how speaking this truth can lift you up inside. Ask how the other person is feeling, too. Notice how your acknowledgment might impact their response.

Practices and Prompts

STOP. LOOK. GO. PRACTICE
Welcome Possibility for the Body

Allow your body to soften, wherever it is, exactly as it is. Open to the possibility of appreciation and ease in relationship to your physical self. Commit to feeling everything gently. You may want to take a few moments to sit or lie down, resting comfortably, feeling supported. You can experiment with putting your hand, or both hands, on your chest. Let yourself notice, really notice, your heart beating and your lungs breathing.

Stop: Enjoy the opportunity to devote your attention to being still. Become conscious of your breath. Follow a complete inhale-exhale cycle with your full awareness.

Look: Focus on how much is happening in your body every moment without your effort, without your having to try to make anything happen. Hold the idea that — no matter what else might feel true — your body is nothing short of spectacular. You are more than any one part; you are even more than the sum of all your parts. Your body is a precious vessel. You are alive right now, and that is a fact to be treasured.

Go: Write down three things about your body that are working and for which you feel grateful. Whenever your mind slips into negative thoughts, interrupt the pattern by reminding yourself of these three things, saying to yourself: I am grateful for my body. Focus on everything that *is* functioning well.

Create a physical gesture of tenderness and care, such as placing your hand on your heart, to offer yourself if you get stuck in judgment. When you are caught in what feels wrong, let this gesture be a healing reminder to your body that it is deeply appreciated and that you hold yourself with tenderness.

Embody Gratitude

Take a few slow breaths as you settle into a seated position. As you become more internally quiet, close your eyes and imagine sitting with gratitude and reverence for your body. See yourself embodying a posture that totally treasures your body, exactly as it is. What does it look like? How does it feel? Make adjustments in the way that you are sitting so as to occupy this embodiment of gratitude. Where do your hands want to be placed? How is your spine? Does your head change position? Experiment with subtle shifts until you find a posture that reflects a treasuring of your body. Take a few more breaths and notice what arises. Open your eyes and offer yourself some appreciation.

As you observe and experience your body throughout the day, try to let it move gratefully. How does gratitude change how your carry and hold your body? Notice what unfolds within you and around you when you commit to embody gratitude.

PERSPECTIVE PROMPTS
Both Broken and Whole

Our bodies are alive, and we have no idea how long this is going to be true. We live every day inside this great mystery, and yet it is extremely challenging to acknowledge regularly. Denying or ignoring the fact of our impermanence keeps us from the work of befriending our body. Our body deserves to be treasured, now. It wants to be celebrated as it is — broken *and* whole. We give ourselves an irreplaceable gift when we praise our body every day as our temporary, extraordinary temple that offers the gift of being alive.

Let yourself be drawn into the poignancy of your body in this moment. It carries you with such generosity and commitment in the face of all its unknowns. Live as a celebration of this love.

✳

I gratefully celebrate the extraordinary home of my body.

Know You Are Kin

No matter how much separates or differentiates us, everyone alive right now has a physical form, one that experiences suffering and pleasure and all manner of sensation: a body that makes everything possible, and yet a body for which much is impossible. The body unites us in the magnitude of our amazing similarities. No matter how different we are from each other, we are connected through our breath, our hearts beating, and all the systems that support us in being alive. No matter what distinguishes us, our bodies invite us to know each other as kin.

Feel yourself nestled in the embrace of the universe — that which holds you among all people throughout time — as an embodiment of life-force.

✳

My body is a unique expression, connecting me with all of humanity.

Reframe Your Suffering

When we revere life, we can better appreciate all that is extraordinary, functioning, and whole about our bodies. We celebrate what works, knowing it could always be otherwise. Staying mindful of the suffering of others can help us reframe our own. And what our body has endured may be the exact reframe that someone else needs to gain perspective. We are each other's teachers, keepers, healers. Appreciative of our own scars, we can be respectful of the wounds of others. It has been wisely said: *Be kind, for everyone you meet is fighting a hard battle.*

Allow yourself to feel grateful for the countless aspects of your body that are working exquisitely in every moment. Notice all the good fortune you enjoy through your body, right now.

✳

I gratefully acknowledge the countless privileges and gifts of my body.

Live Your Values

Many of us espouse strongly principled commitments to well-being and health. We say we care about and appreciate our physical selves. And yet there may be great dissonance between what we say and where we actually put our time, attention, and energy. You will be well served to be clear about what you value about your body and then find ways to remember and act in alignment with these core beliefs. Living with appreciation and integrity enhances your perspective.

Clarify your values and principles about your body. Write them down. What guides you? Hold this guidance close whenever you tend your body.

✳

I am aligned with clear values that guide a loving relationship with my body.

Delight in Your Senses

As physical beings, we use our senses to experience life. How often do you find yourself sleepwalking through a day, and then catch sight of something, a beautiful bird, flower, or smiling face, and your heart wakes up? The sound of your favorite music can crack you open. A certain smell or taste can make buried memories surface. The power of our senses to stir an archeology of positive sensation and memory is profound. These pleasures can be potent medicine, especially if you have been wounded by pain or illness.

Remember your senses and how they deliver pleasure and blessing for yourself and others. Sharing gifts that open the senses moves the heart of both giver and receiver to joy.

✳

I appreciate my body's tenacious ability to discover and know pleasure.

CHAPTER 6

APPRECIATING OUR EMOTIONS

On Fears and Fearlessness

My cancer diagnosis came in the early 1990s when the New Age movement was in full swing, bringing its beliefs to bear on the growing populations of people living with AIDS and cancer. *Love, Medicine, and Miracles* by Bernie Siegel, and Louise Hay's *You Can Heal Your Life* were bestsellers. The ideas that everything happens for a predetermined reason and that we can be entirely in control of what happens to us translated into far-reaching theories about how our thoughts and feelings are both the cause and cure for illness. According to this popular train of thought, if you wanted to heal a disobedient body, you simply needed to work on your disobedient mind. Death was essentially regarded as a failure of will. If you got sick, it was because you had not done the right things to heal your wrong outlooks. If you died, it was because you did not want to live.

I was no stranger to these ideas. As a young adult, I was an idealist with an allegiance to nontraditional lifestyles and alternative medicine, and many New Age ideas appealed to me. As far as I was concerned, our capacity for self-determination and self-healing made sense, and I was convinced I could treat any illness that came my way with a combination of macrobiotic diet, vitamins, and optimism. Then I was hit with an advanced cancer diagnosis and the prescription of a new, aggressive, conventional Western-medicine chemotherapy protocol. I started seeing people around me get sick, suffer, and die no matter their lifestyle or treatment path — children, young moms, dear friends, spiritual teachers — all of whom loved life and were committed to physical and psychological health. It was then that I was forced to reconcile my beliefs to a more complex reality.

The notion that staying alive would require a relentlessly positive attitude was a hard prescription to shake. Though it surely made sense to feel sad, scared, and upset given what I was going through, I thought that allowing myself to feel these things was a one-way ticket to my downfall, a death sentence. I kept getting caught in a downward spiral: I would feel sad, then scared that I was sad, then upset that I was scared about being sad. Fear of my fear became terror. Sadness about my sadness became depression. And being upset about being upset made me feel doomed.

My former therapist reappeared in my life to help me navigate these treacherous emotional waters. She offered me the support to notice and name my emotions, grant them space and acceptance, and observe how they would soften and pass if I did not judge them. The feelings of sadness and fear did not need to define me, nor were they my enemy. Trusting my feelings and facing them with appreciative curiosity made them no longer scary or overwhelming. They only became tenacious when I questioned their right to exist. This held true even when I faced the prospect of my own death.

My emotional landscape was one of intense vulnerability. Befriending it with respect and compassion mattered immensely to my well-being. I came to see vulnerability as the nature of the human experience, connecting me to lovability and belonging — not separating me from people. I suddenly saw that everyone had cracks where, as Leonard Cohen says, "the light gets in." We were traveling in our tenderness together. Putting out the welcome mat for vulnerability became central to my healing.

I spent months during and after treatment unwinding the belief that having certain thoughts or feelings was going to keep me sick or even bring about my demise. The cultural messages vilifying negative emotions did not abate, but trusting that I needed my whole self to come with me into wellness, I had to assume that whatever thoughts and feelings showed up had meaning. I had already learned so much from life, and I did not want to dishonor any parts of myself — so I became curious about them instead. With time and committed practice, I became more able to turn toward sadness, fear, or upset whenever it arose, look at it directly, hold it with interest and compassion, and allow its wisdom to guide me.

THE VALUE OF VULNERABILITY

We are never more than one grateful thought away from peace of heart.
— Brother David Steindl-Rast

Emotions, feelings, and the thoughts that accompany them come and go like the weather. Some days, a solitary emotion seems to be our only companion. Some days we run through a whole, wild bevy of emotional weather systems between waking and sleep. And while it is we who have feelings, and ideas about those feelings, sometimes it can feel like they "have" us.

Feelings and emotions simply are. Like the breath, they are a constant. Humans have anywhere from 6 to 27 basic emotions, and hundreds of feelings, all interconnected. We can know our feelings through the somatic portal of the body, and through the cognitive portal of the mind, but many people see them as emanating from the figurative space of the heart. Some believe we experience our emotions through feelings; some see it in reverse. Emotions are essential responses to our conditions; they can be as fleeting and fascinating as clouds or sunlight. But we often approach this rugged landscape with much trepidation. With loaded histories and loads of uncertainties, we embark on our emotional journeys laden and unsettled, afraid of what might be around the next bend, or the steep climb that seems it might never end.

The word *emotion* literally means "energy in motion." Emotions move us to make messes, to make love, to make change, to make art. These actions create ripples of new emotions. Even if we endure a prolonged emotional or mental state such as depression or anxiety, these experiences have nuances; we notice glimpses of distinct feelings if we offer our interested attention. As with Impressionist paintings, when we move in close to our internal landscape, we see thousands of small brush strokes. So, too, are our feelings rich with a variety of hues and textures when we regard them with close and curious scrutiny.

Gratefulness supports us as we seek to befriend our emotions with a gentler and more inclusive perspective. Vulnerability will be close at hand and heart when we do this — it is often directly behind or underneath many of the feelings that we present to the world. When we note the surprising emotional nuances on the path we are traveling, the opportunity to suffer less and learn more is available to us — as well as the opportunity to more fully enjoy the journey.

BECOME PRESENT TO YOUR EMOTIONS

The best and most beautiful things in life cannot be seen or even touched.
They must be felt with the heart. — Helen Keller

Graciously coexisting with our emotions is the precondition for much of what
we long for: Self-awareness. Insight. Personal agency. Equanimity. Empathy.
Intimacy. If you want to live a more grateful life — and enjoy its rich rewards —
you cannot bypass joining forces with the great fullness of your emotions.

Practicing mindfulness reminds us of our ability to pay attention to our
internal experiences, on purpose, without judgment. Mindfulness helps us to
not get carried away by a story we tell ourselves about an emotion — about
how a feeling is good or bad, shameful, or worthwhile. The essential insight
that emotions and feelings come and go, and that we may have thoughts about
them, but they do not "have" us, can spark a small revolution. Mindful presence slows us down, allows for greater acceptance and self-compassion, and
softens our feelings of being overwhelmed.

One reason to become more gratefully present to our emotions is to learn
to value whatever arises. We know that resistance generates persistence and
suppression generates suffering. We need to strengthen our musculature for
being with our feelings as they are, honoring their offerings and guidance.
Practicing being present with an emotion allows it to have its arrival, its
nuanced impact, and its departure. In the gracious space of regarding an emotion with attention and curiosity, we can experience more appreciation for the
great fullness of who — and how — we are.

Mindfulness makes us aware, and gratefulness wakes us up to notice
the gifts within and around us. Once we have paused to take in the present
moment, a grateful perspective invites us to extend our attention to whatever
is waiting in the wings: The richness of our hearts. The beauty of our tenderness. The intelligence of our feelings, all of them.

✳

What is an emotion you experience often and welcome with open
arms? When you embrace it fully, what other emotions come with it?

✳

What are some ways you could invite yourself to be more curious
and compassionate when your emotions are challenging?

VOICES OF GRATEFUL LIVING

Life is full of ups and downs. I know that, but when the hard times come my energy gets pulled down like things will be like this forever. If I want to stay more centered and able to balance this energy, I find things to be grateful for. It helps to establish the truth of impermanence. It raises my energy and connects me to a more life-giving field. It is an effort for me, and I am so grateful I have gratefulness to get through the bumps that come. — Mary B.

SEEK A PERSPECTIVE OF COMPASSION AND CURIOSITY

When you feel yourself breaking down, may you break open instead. May every experience in life be a door that opens your heart, expands your understanding, and leads you to freedom. — Elizabeth Lesser

It is understandable and wholly human to prefer certain feelings over others. Some are far more tolerable or comfortable. How we orient to our lives through our most common emotions is highly individual, and even dispositional or constitutional. How we experience, integrate, and express our feelings as they arise — that is what makes us unique. But having a deep emotional life that challenges and enriches us and brings us into an experience of vulnerability — this universal truth is what makes us human. And it is the source of our most gratifying connections with all other humans.

We get into trouble when we embed our feelings into strict categories: good, bad, right, wrong. This categorizing is the mind's attempt to bring a sense of order to a terrain that it often finds inefficient and disorderly. When our mind is meddlesome and controlling, as soon as a feeling arises it wants to classify it, especially if it is uncomfortable; the mind has little patience for discomfort. So we judge it. Label it. Compare it. Shame it. Hide it. Create a story about it. We tell ourselves this emotion might last forever, or get worse. We believe our feelings will make us either lovable or unlovable. This is how our minds make a target out of our tender hearts.

When we can quiet the mind — or at least make it more of an interested observer — and hold our tenderness with compassion, we can more readily harvest the riches of our emotional lives. Here, we get to behold the potency of our feelings and the exquisite truth of our humanity. Embracing our vulnerability allows our emotional experiences the space to inform and transform us. "Vulnerability is not weakness," says social science researcher Brené Brown. "Vulnerability is the birthplace of innovation, creativity and change." To dismiss vulnerability is to deny our authenticity, impairing our ability to develop ourselves and authentic connections with others.

Grateful living helps us become more compassionate, curious, and even celebratory about our emotional lives. It helps us see that our vulnerability is the key which unlocks the door to what we are longing for in life. Grateful living can offer powerful reframes and redirection for our attention when we feel emotionally overwhelmed or isolated. And we can work *with* our habits of mind, as opposed to against them, learning from awareness of our moment-to-moment feelings and thoughts.

✻

How does vulnerability help you feel a heightened sense of
connection in your emotional life or your relationships?

✻

What is one emotion that can be challenging to embrace?
What term of endearment could you give this emotion
so when it arrives, it has a character you can welcome
with tender recognition?

AWAKEN POSSIBILITY FOR THE COLLECTIVE HEART

As they become known to and accepted by us, our feelings and the honest exploration of them become sanctuaries and spawning grounds for the most radical and daring of ideas. — Audre Lorde

Our emotional lives can keep us myopic — sometimes out of the necessity for growth and healing, and sometimes because fear limits and hampers us. When we open the lens to see ourselves as part of the world and related to others through our struggles, our emotional energies become more available. We find rejuvenation of our compassion for others in our human family, for all creatures, and for the Earth. Recognizing that the suffering of one person is the suffering of all, we are compelled to know we must carry each other across the rugged landscape of life, and trust we will be carried in the process.

When our emotional self-acceptance is turned on and our blinders are off, we recognize opportunities everywhere. We can see needs everywhere, calling for our care and engagement. We know we are a vital part of this beautiful constellation, and we advance toward those opportunities, perfectly messy, perfectly needy, and perfectly enough. It is not necessary to wait until we feel suitably strong and emotionally complete to begin listening; it is these exact conditions that make us best able to serve the world and our own development simultaneously.

When our hearts are awakened to our feelings, and our feelings are awakened to guide us, we can situate ourselves in a landscape of belonging. How we perceive the whole world changes when we tune in to vulnerability and brokenness as a shared experience, not ours alone. We can step outside of our singularity and discover ourselves accompanied. It is in these resonant moments we find our calling to be of service to a larger universe. Moved to tend to the collective heart, we know we are tending to our own.

Our world awaits your heart's full employment, not its perfect composure. Your heart awaits the wake-up call of this moment, fully embraced and fully loved for all of its broken beauty. Let wholeheartedness turn you toward the possibility that wants to be awakened in you.

✳

What emotions move me toward action?

✳

How does being grateful for my vulnerability support me to see and
create greater possibility in my life and in the world?

VOICES OF GRATEFUL LIVING

For me living wholeheartedly means to have the courage to create the life I want from the vision of my heart. There is a great deal of risk and high level of vulnerability associated with this, but I know it is my only path to a life that will fully manifest all of my deepest heart's desires. I take courageous steps toward this daily. — Kathryn L.

LAUGHTER
When the
face we wear
grows old and weathered, torn
open by time,
colors
tinted as dawn
like the late
winter mountains
of Sedona
ashen and crimson.
It will no longer
be possible
to distinguish
our deepest scars
from the long
sweet lines left
by laughter.
— Dale Biron

GRATEFUL FOR EACH MOMENT

Clouds come floating into my life from other days no longer to shed rain
or usher storm but to give colour to my sunset sky. — Rabindranath Tagore

Like our bodies, our emotions offer abundant opportunities to practice bringing gratefulness to life. We have a perpetual invitation to embrace ourselves unconditionally. Accepting and celebrating the value of vulnerability, we are set free to better enjoy the blessings inside and all around us. Here. Now. Always.

Grateful living invites us to know that our emotions are our true riches. The ability to feel deeply and respond fully to life is an unparalleled blessing. Loving with our hearts wide open and with the capacity to be "undone" by love and compassion — this supports our full humanness. To want anything other than this would be a travesty to our potential and to our world. Accepting and appreciating our emotional lives is a big yes to life.

✳

May you hold all your feelings with compassion and curiosity.

Practices and Prompts

STOP. LOOK. GO. PRACTICE
Embrace the Possibilities of Your Emotional Life

Being able to identify and embrace the nuances of our feelings is hugely liberating. There is good news in the fact that we can feel anything at all. It is really good news that we are tenderhearted and capable of feeling, even things we might not like to feel. It means we are human. And being human is a big, vulnerable job.

> **Stop:** Offer your attention to being still or slowing down. Bring your awareness to the present moment and allow yourself to sink into it. Put your hand on your heart. Focus on your breath while letting your heart soften.

> **Look:** Turn your attention to how you are feeling right now. The first thing that arises is often a story to explain your feelings, but underneath that story are other important feelings. Can you get past the story to at least one feeling, clearly? Does it arise with a name? Try naming it softly.

> Now can you approach this feeling with the same kind of curiosity you might offer a child who is hurting? Can you picture bending down and offering eye contact and your full attention? Can you cultivate tenderness? Are there layers underneath the feeling? Explore its edges and girth. What is the texture? Listen to the physical sensations that arrive with these feelings. Be receptive to this wisdom. Ask how your heart would describe its current state. With kindness, allow more "feeling" words to come to mind. Speak them softly as they arise. Just as the color red can be crimson, scarlet, rose, or ruby, anger can also have shades of frustration, fear, impatience, insecurity, or resentment.

Invite yourself to imagine a range of nuanced names that you could use to describe one of your feelings.

Go: Your emotions are each points of light, illuminating your path and simultaneously the paths of others. Embrace how full of light you are. Notice that you can be compassionate toward your emotions and that compassion can change the quality of your attention for other people and their struggles.

From the fullness of your compassionate heart, extend yourself with kindness to someone in need today. Act with generosity. Tend a hurt you might be able to help heal. It is amazing how easy it is to make someone's day with an act of kindness, and it is remarkable how much a focus on helping others can ripple back, helping us feel more connected and at ease.

Emotions as Energy in Motion

Close your eyes and take a few deep breaths. Notice an emotion that is in the background of your direct attention, a feeling asking for recognition. Invite it into your awareness and welcome it by name: "Hello, __." Simply acknowledging and naming our feelings can help them soften and have less of a charge. Practice greeting this same feeling by name with each exhale until another feeling enters your awareness. Welcome it in as you gently allow the first emotion to move on. Notice and appreciate that feelings are always in motion, all the more so when we acknowledge them and let them go.

Serving Vulnerability

Consider the ways your vulnerability could be a gift to others. Who needs to know that their vulnerability does not separate them from the rest of the world? Think of ways that you could share your vulnerability in support of an individual, group, or population in need. Tell your story. Offer yourself in service. Make a commitment to show up in places where the truth of vulnerability is a shared norm — for people struggling with addictions, mental health issues, poverty, illness, human tenderness.

PERSPECTIVE PROMPTS
Treat Your Feelings with Hospitality

As we nourish our relationship with uncertainty and vulnerability, we are more in touch with poignancy. This poignancy makes it easier to see our emotions as energy in motion, passing into and through our lives laden with gifts — if we open our doors, our arms, our hearts. We can be more readily moved by what arrives when we know that no feeling lasts, no visitation is forever. We have no idea how long we will get to have any of our feelings. Holding them lightly, with respect, curiosity, and compassion, assures them they have been seen.

Experiment with treating all your feelings with equal hospitality, knowing that they have gifts for you in this moment, and may never come again.

✳

My entire emotional landscape is in service of a wholehearted life.

Difficult Emotions Make You Who You Are

If we open the lens on our life, we will see that there is no feeling we have not experienced in some form before. And survived. Or enjoyed. Mostly learned from, if we have allowed ourselves to take in its teachings. Each has made us who we are now. The surprises faced with courage, the pain met with tenderness, the challenges held with faith — all delivering us into greater aliveness. Vulnerability and love embraced with reverence — greater fullness. When we look back on our lives, we see that it is often our most challenging emotional experiences that burnished us into brighter shining.

Remind yourself of tough situations and emotions that you did not expect but that made you who you are. Know that you will be able to look back on current struggles with appreciation for their teachings.

✳

My emotions bring valuable lessons, and I invite them into my life.

Variety Is a Blessing

We can learn to regard our feelings as serving us most when they are diversified, when our emotional landscape contains a range of terrains — all extraordinary. Variety is a blessing. The wider our capacities, the more resourceful we can be in all areas of our lives. The more we can adapt and accommodate, the more resilient we are. The more emotions we can encounter and befriend, the more riches we have to bring to our lives and the lives of others. Imagine how diminished we would be with only a single emotion through which to experience life.

Consider your emotions a privilege, each one able to bring richness to the landscape of your life when greeted with appreciation.

✳

I am blessed by the wide range of my feelings, each one a gift.

Treat Yourself as You Would Treat Others

We sometimes give our best advice to people when they are facing challenging emotions. Often our best selves rise to the occasion, and what we hold as sacred can be shared. We speak from the heart of our true beliefs and we offer kindness and compassion to others. If we are able to turn this same sacred appreciation toward ourselves, we can align with what we stand for. Excluding ourselves from the attentive emotional care that we give others takes us out of integrity; including ourselves is an embodiment of gratefulness.

Make a real effort to give yourself the focused emotional attention that you offer others. Your well-being will benefit greatly when you tend yourself with such appreciation and care.

✳

My compassion is sacred, and I direct it toward myself when I need it.

Absorb All the Goodness

If you make an effort to deepen the nourishment that comes from enjoyable experiences, you will be better able to bring your strengths in service of the challenging times in life. Instead of distracting yourself from a pleasurable moment, go into super-soak mode and absorb every bit of its goodness. Let the blessings of a pleasurable moment saturate your cells. Occupy it fully. Create such a powerful reservoir of pleasure that it can carry you through challenging times. Fill your cup to the brim so that there is nourishment for the times when you need it.

When you find yourself having an experience that magnifies grateful feelings, turn up the dial to super-soak, become even more porous, don't hold back, take it all in.

✻

I allow myself to lean fully into the pleasing moments in my life.

CHAPTER 7

BEFRIENDING OUR FULL SELVES

Trust Where It Matters

A cancer diagnosis can unleash steady waves of well-intentioned opinions and advice. In my case, it felt like a tsunami. Friends, family, strangers, and professionals from near and far shared suggestions about the latest magic-bullet medicine, prayers, doctors, herbs, healers, supplements, research, books, clinical trials, and alternative treatments. Many of their recommendations required plane travel, large sums of money, or abandonment of the chemotherapy regimen I had begun. All required leaps of faith when I was already in midair. Every day someone suggested something they thought might increase the odds of my survival. All of it was offered with love and hope. All of it was overwhelming.

It was especially challenging to know what to do, as I did not tolerate my chemotherapy protocol well. After my first infusion, both my weight and white blood cell count dropped precipitously, and I was informed I would need to begin giving myself daily injections to make it through. Keeping to the schedule, I was told, was of paramount importance. My spinal fusion — only four weeks old when chemo started — did not take well to the treatment either, and after the second infusion I found myself back in a wheelchair.

Traveling down a treatment path that departed significantly from anything I had ever imagined, and then suffering from it, I fell prey to bouts of doubt about how and whether to keep to the plan. I was constantly weighing and sampling complementary treatments. I was vulnerable, scared, and in physical distress: the perfect conditions to make me susceptible to external influences. Not wanting to close the door on any option that held promise, I flirted with every possibility.

Around the time of my third chemo infusion, sicker than I had ever been, I got a call from an old high school classmate. He, too, was coping with a lymphoma diagnosis, but his doctors had put him on a different chemo protocol. He was further down the treatment path and doing well. He recommended a treatment center in Florida, antioxidant vitamins, and a couple of books, and he suggested I never let myself have a single thought about the possibility of dying. Then he told me that he knew someone who had been on the chemo regimen I was receiving, but she had recently passed away.

Hitting emotional bottom is a hard fall. But it also offers us something concrete against which to push and generate upward momentum. This conversation thrust me to the ground and left my head spinning. How was I meant to process all the information coming my way? How could I weigh all the options available and offered? How could I reconcile the contradictory information I was getting? How could I take other people's ideas to heart and still take care of myself? I quickly realized that I couldn't, and that was a good thing.

With the stakes so high, it became clear that I had succumbed to other people's fears and become frantic for answers. I had put my mind in charge, and my mind (as well as everyone else's) wanted more and more information and options. I had lost connection with my internal guidance system. When I tried to consider my choices without being centered in my heart and checking them against my intuition, I lost my balance altogether. Even though it felt like I owed people consideration of their ideas, there was nothing better I could offer than my own instincts and clarity. This meant establishing deeper and more consistent ways of attuning and listening to myself, and establishing better boundaries with others. I needed to own my journey, and I could help others let go of trying to save me by standing assuredly on my own feet and in my own inner knowing. It was clear that any effective way forward was going to depend on my ability to cultivate, source, and trust my own wisdom — no matter what the results might be.

AN INITIATION TO LOVE AND BELONGING

Nothing gives more joy than when your heart grows wider and wider and your sense of belonging to the universe grows deeper and deeper.
— Brother David Steindl-Rast

Thinking of gratitude in transactional terms makes us inclined to be grateful to others, and for external gifts and blessings. But in an effort to live gratefully in our relationships with others, it is best to begin by developing kindness and appreciation toward ourselves. This helps us reinforce gratefulness as an inside job.

The ways in which we do and do not relate attentively to ourselves are complex and beg for deeper exploration. Embedded in a culture that drives us to fixate on how we present ourselves for social approval, many of us are left with inner lives that feel malnourished. Our capacity to offer true appreciation and consideration to others is hampered if we do not also turn our attention toward ourselves, for exactly who and where we are. We must learn to deepen our self-trust before we can extend trust to others.

Living gratefully, we are called to act from the knowledge that simply because we are here, we are essential in the world. You are the precious portal through which love and life are given and received. You are both the source and the connection to a more infinite source — and deepening the robustness of this connection deepens your entire sense of relatedness. We can spend much of our lives longing and searching for belonging, and looking to others to fill us up. Meanwhile, we come home to ourselves in every moment, replete with the blessings of unparalleled kinship. If we listen, the universe reassures us of our true home within the larger constellation of everything. And all the while, we belong to love and life, and life and love belong to us.

VOICES OF GRATEFUL LIVING

Gratitude as a way of being enables me to get out of my own way in seeing that I am not the main player in the universe. It broadens my sense of belonging to things beyond me, reconnects me to deeper parts of myself that were neglected. This feeds a feeling of sufficiency. — Alan D.

BECOME PRESENT TO WHO YOU ARE

You are loved just for being who you are, just for existing. You don't have to do anything to earn it. No one can take this love away from you, and it will always be here. — Ram Dass

The practice of intentional self-appreciation is cultivated in the present moment. As is. As we are. Appreciation invites us to be fully present to what is "so," and then to lean in with an open heart. When we direct attention toward ourselves, the present moment asks us to surrender the burden of the incessant goals, striving, and our need for accomplishment. We honor each moment when we release the litany of ideas about what might be required before we can be grateful for who we are: all those unfulfilled resolutions; things we think we need to have, be, or fix; and people whose permission or approval we think we should await. There are no preconditions for self-befriending. We can even set down the confining ways we have learned to identify ourselves in the world. You do not need to do, have, or be anything to be worthy of receiving your own acceptance and kindness. Instead, you can turn toward yourself, extending a more merciful appreciation for every aspect of who you are, exactly as you are. All of it. Here. Now.

It is human — and culturally encouraged — to want to work on, change, refine, and try to "better" ourselves, always aiming toward some yet-to-be and might-never-be future. But before we undertake any efforts toward self-improvement, we must first compassionately accept ourselves for the fullness and truth of who we are; acknowledge the courageous, circuitous path we took to get here; and recognize that it is all actually enough. We are served by approaching ourselves with a sweeping and inclusive embrace of the many qualities we may be inclined to judge or disavow. The exiled parts. The pathologized ways of being. The marginalized feelings. The hidden hurts. The tender sensitivities. You discover a gracious capacity for empathy when you learn to lean into yourself with the embrace of a close friend. And then, ironically, many of the things you have long wanted to "better" become compassionately integrated into a more beloved sense of self. You are the ever-available focus for your own loving exploration, and the unconditional consideration you so readily offer, and long for, from others.

Our capacity for gratefulness will depend heartily on the depth of companionship we offer ourselves. Learning to be present, we recognize that self-befriending will take us a very long way down the road of leading more grateful lives, and so we turn toward a more sacred partnership.

✳

What aspects of yourself are you most at ease sharing with the world?

✳

What aspects of yourself have you made less welcome? How might
you offer yourself more inclusive appreciation?

SEEK A PERSPECTIVE OF SELF-APPRECIATION AND TRUST

Self-trust is the first secret of success. — Ralph Waldo Emerson

The recognition that the shared human condition is one of vulnerability can offer great perspective and peace: the ways in which we see ourselves as broken or deficient are sadly more common than not. Many of us feel isolated and "other," and then feel more other for feeling other, or feel bad for feeling bad. Fear of not doing enough translates into not *being* enough. Doing something wrong can make us feel there is something wrong with us or that we are wholly wrong. The practice of gratefully intervening in these self-judgments with unconditional acceptance, appreciation, and compassion — even celebration — is the path of self-befriending.

Let's approach the practice of grateful self-befriending as a big step on the path toward unconditional love. We may place healthy conditions on our love for others, and we will surely have conditional terms for our relationships, but with ourselves we can experience the biggest possible playground of "unconditional." If we hold our vulnerabilities and sensitivities as rich sources of information about how we deserve and need to be treated — not things that need to be changed — and if we honor ourselves with compassionate care, we can forge an abiding friendship that will deliver blessings in every aspect of life. This gracious space we make for ourselves will inform the space we invite others to occupy as well.

Renowned for his successful marriage counseling practice, Dr. John Gottman has brought tangible tools to the aid of thousands of couples who have longed for more intimate relationships. According to Gottman, one of the harbingers of a fruitful union is our capacity to accept influence from our partner, meaning that we readily accept, respect, and are willing to be impacted by their perspective. Among its many benefits, accepting influence establishes and increases humility and nondefensiveness, openness to new ways of seeing things, and cooperation.

A nurturing partnership with yourself can deliver wiser counsel than any outside influence. It places the value of trust where it is most helpful and lasting — within you. When you commit to deepening your self-trust, you seek and heed the intimacy of your own influence. You forge an intentional union with your insights and gut instincts. You listen for that still, small voice within, and rely on a reliable source: your intuition. Listening to inner wisdom and accepting your own influence is an act of compassionate self-befriending that will help to carry you everywhere, and through everything.

❋

What does your intuition tell you it needs in order to be a trustworthy source of wisdom? How does your intuition want to be consulted, treated, and heeded?

❋

What are some qualities in yourself you have judged that you could instead appreciate as lovable quirks?

AWAKEN POSSIBILITY FOR YOURSELF

Trust is the active engagement with the unknown. Trust is risky. It's vulnerable. It's a leap of faith. . . . The more we trust, the farther we are able to venture. — Esther Perel

Given that gratefulness is not transactional but is an orientation to life that emanates from inside us, we can embrace the idea that being grateful in all of our relationships is fundamentally sourced, practiced, and burnished from within — through the moment-to-moment ways we relate to ourselves and our experiences of life.

With enough presence and perspective, we see that love may be unconditional, but relationships are not. If someone who treats you poorly, knows what hurts you and does it anyway, disrespects your needs, does not accept your influence or care for your vulnerabilities — this may be a relationship or a situation to walk away from. And if the person mistreating you and ignoring your needs is *you*, wrap yourself in compassion as you stop yourself in your own tracks — it is due time for self-befriending. Walk out the door of self-judgment and down the path of compassionate self-appreciation . . . now.

Possibility is awakened, or not, every day through how we treat ourselves. Without the strength of grateful self-regard, possibility in any area is going to be circumscribed by our internalized limitations. We cannot know what is possible with others or with life until we give ourselves permission for a more unlimited and grateful experience of ourselves.

✳

If you were to stop waiting and treat yourself exactly as you long to, what new opportunities would arise?

✳

How might appreciating the greatest fullness of who you are right now invite you to act differently in the world? What might it inspire?

VOICES OF GRATEFUL LIVING

I spend long hours in service professionally and as a volunteer, both of which I value and for which I am grateful. Frequently, though, I find myself feeling depleted, and gratefulness reflections serve to help restore my strength. I have been reframing my perspective to recognize that self-worth is not a zero-sum game. There is no "best" but instead one in which the world is enriched by focusing on bringing our personal, unique, best self forward. When I come to my work with that perspective, I give more fully and freely. It allows me to bring my best self to both my profession and volunteer work, no longer focusing on how I perform, but instead on what I can give. — Lisa B.

RETHINKING REGRET

Let's thank our mistakes, let's bless them
for their humanity, their terribly weak chins.
We should offer them our gratitude and admiration
for giving us our clefts and scarring us with
embarrassment, the hot flash of confession.
Thank you, transgressions! for making us so right
in our imperfections. Less flawed, we might have
turned away, feeling too fit, our desires looking
for better directions. Without them, we might have
passed the place where one of us stood, watching
someone else walk away, and followed them,
while our perfect mistake walked straight toward us,
walked right into our cluttered, ordered lives
that could have been closed but were not,
that could have been asleep, but instead
stayed up, all night, forgetting the pill,
the good book, the necessary eight hours,
and lay there — in the middle of the bed —
keeping the heart awake — open and stunned,
stunning. How unhappy perfection must be
over there on the shelf without a crack, without
this critical break — this falling — this sudden, thrilling draft.
— Elaine Sexton

GRATEFUL FOR EACH MOMENT

Nothing can dim the light that shines from within. — Maya Angelou

When we seek a deeper experience of love and belonging, we are called to step away from the scales of self-scrutiny and appraisal, to move away from the magnifying mirror of self-judgment into which we so often look. We remember that our essence cannot be compartmentalized. Our essential nature asks for a wider lens within a much larger, more grateful context — that of the grand human family, across continents and across generations, united in vulnerability and connected in belonging.

Grateful living helps us to deepen a sacred connection with ourselves, as we are. When we welcome the varied terrain of experience within us, the opportunities and gifts of insight and intimacy are endless. When we practice being grateful for who we are and how we are, wherever we are, we cultivate a reservoir of self-trust — a touchstone we can return to again and again for nourishment and guidance.

May you hold yourself with self-appreciation and trust.

Practices and Prompts

STOP. LOOK. GO. PRACTICE
Remember Your Joyful Self

Think back to when you were between 7 and 12 years old. This is a period in life when you developed important aspects of your social and emotional identity. This is also a time when you solidify meaningful forms of self-accompaniment. Think about some things you did when you "spent" yourself fully but were filled to overflowing by the activity, something you could do for hours and lose all sense of time. Maybe it was playing a game, reading, writing, solving a puzzle, painting, drawing, playing music, hiking in nature, building or making things, dancing, playing a sport, or creating anything.

A joyful activity in your youth is surely something that aroused gratefulness in you, and it may be calling to be reexplored or explored in a new way that honors any current limitations you have. Oftentimes as kids we can be happy for hours in only our own company. We can call on this self-befriending later in life, too.

> **Stop:** Offer your attention to being still or slowing down. Bring your awareness to the present moment and allow yourself to sink into it. Put both hands on your chest. Focus on your breath while letting your heart soften.

> **Look:** Fix your memory on one activity that engaged and delighted you fully as a child. Focus on how it made your mind, body, and emotions feel to be engaged in this activity. Feel those

same sensations coming to life in you now as you remember this part of your life. What activity so absorbed your attention as a kid that you would lose track of time? Something that so fully engrossed your senses that you would not hear someone calling you? Something you loved to do so much that you were "all in"? Write down what this inquiry brings to the surface for you now.

Go: Reinvigorating the things we most loved to do when we were young can be a very energizing grateful living practice. We can gain great benefit from making a commitment to bring more exploration, play, and creativity into our lives, and we discover ways these gifts can bring us into connection with, or help us serve, others. There may be opportunities for you to volunteer or get involved with others engaged in this activity — or start a group of your own. Pursue the things that take you "all in" — and that bring your heart alive.

Trust Your Intuition

Sit quietly with your eyes closed. Take a few full breaths. Place your awareness on the part of your belly where you might experience a "gut instinct" or an "intuitive hit." This may be just above or below your belly button, or just under your rib cage. Place both of your hands there as you breathe into stillness. Now ask: "What do I need right now?" Try not to think your way to an answer. Tune in to inner knowing and let your body's wisdom speak. It can be a subtle and slow communication, or it might be immediate and vivid. Either way, listen to what surfaces. Your intuition is a deep fount of intelligence available to you.

If you want to continue your exploration, ask yourself, "How can I best meet this need?" or "Is there a deeper need underneath?" Say "Thank you" when you receive a clear message. Trust depends on appreciation. Write down any insights before you transition into "doing" anything. Consider using this practice throughout the day when you are seeking clarity. Trusting your intuition is not the same as consulting a crystal ball. Be sure to ask "I" questions of your inner knowing; in doing so, you activate greater self-awareness.

Give Yourself Gratefully

When we relate to ourselves generously, there is far more of our-selves to offer as time and energy previously spent in various forms of mistrust and mistreatment of ourselves become available to unleash. Choose one way you can be of service this week, and do it fully and gratefully, feeling blessed by the opportunity to give. Listen to your need for self-care, and trust that you will offer it as needed. Watch how much further you can extend yourself and how much more you can give when self-trust and great fullness of heart guide you.

PERSPECTIVE PROMPTS

Behold Yourself as a Newborn

One way to gain perspective is to look at ourselves as if beholding a newborn; our essential nature is so much more available to us in infancy. Babies remind us of the marvel of human life and also its fragility. To become and remain incarnate is nothing short of miraculous. If we can show ourselves the uncon-ditional cherishing we bring to a new life, we can know ourselves anew. It can take our breath away to revel in our magnificence; yes, even in the midst of our messiness. If we allow ourselves a larger field of appreciation, we will come to life more fully.

Let yourself be awestruck by the marvel of your existence. See yourself through eyes of wonder and through the warmth of your own embrace. Pick yourself up with love.

✳

I am a miraculous expression of humanity.

Imagine Your Ancestors

Consider the history that preceded your arrival; we are each the product of millennia of intentionality. Let's honor the energies and intentions of our ancestors toward life. We are the result of so much longing and effort. Our cells are filled with the imprint of generations, and if we could be held by all those who came before us, we would be celebrated so gratefully as perfect — an unimaginable, unrepeatable miracle — exactly as we are. A beautiful surprise.

Imagine yourself at the center of a circle of your ancestors, with their arms outstretched to celebrate you and thank you for carrying on their lineage with such magnificence.

※

My life is a celebration of the longing and energy of all those who came before me.

Give Yourself Credit

It is a radical act to acknowledge how whole and complete we are, especially within a culture bent on trying to convince us that we are not enough. It is a radical act of gratefulness to celebrate all that is abundant and extraordinary about us and our lives. We can give ourselves credit for resilience in the face of lives that are not always easy. We can affirm our courage and strength. We can delight in the idiosyncrasies that are the basis for the love that others feel toward us. And we can be grateful for the conditions that have allowed us to develop our extraordinary strengths.

When you feel lacking, consider all of the ways that you are already enough, and the ways that your ordinary is more than extraordinary.

※

I am cause for celebration, just the way that I am.

Tend to Your Wonders

When we ally ourselves with our innate beliefs and spiritual principles, we are reminded that we are each perfect "children of God." We are made of longing and courage. The world wants us here, now, as we are. Who are we to question this? We were made for purposes that we can spend our entire lifetime exploring. Grace invites us forward to embody ourselves with aplomb and guides us to fulfill our essential being. If you believe in unconditional love, then bring it home to yourself. Tend to your wonders.

Invite yourself to live *as if* — as if you are fully chosen at all times, as if you are aligned with the exact intentions of the universe and your true nature, as if you are imperfectly perfect and perfectly imperfect. You are.

✳

I attend to the ways I wholeheartedly belong.

Be Yourself with Abandon

Our capacity to experience pleasure rests in our ability to be comfortable with who we are. From a place of self-acceptance, we can better notice beauty and celebrate life through all of our senses and see ourselves as an essential part of the whole. We can play, rest, laugh, and be creative with abandon. Abandoning the need to do more and be more opens the doors to the fullness of enjoyment, and enjoyment is a worthy aspiration.

Notice more of the pleasures in being exactly who you are. Embrace your quirks and let them show more, laugh at yourself, and find the occasion to laud your humanity, with love.

✳

I discover joyful pleasure in moments of self-abandon.

CHAPTER 8

CHERISHING CONNECTION

Receiving as an Offering

As a teenager, I was an insatiable giver. "Give big, give early, give often" was my modus operandi. I spent tremendous energy perfecting the craft of anticipating people's needs, rushing in to answer perceived longings, doing more than expected, and always taking less than might be offered. Not surprisingly, I found myself with plenty of willing takers.

Stage IV cancer dramatically shut my "giver" down. Hospitality skills withered. Customary kindnesses died on the vine. My ability to extend myself to others became virtually nonexistent. Friends and family came to visit from around the country, and I could hardly smile at them through my drugged haze. My body was weighted into the bed with pain or nausea, my hands lay like clay at my side, and my eyes glazed over and could hardly stay open. I had never realized how much simple eye contact or touch could be a vital form of generosity and connection until I was unable to offer it.

Still, as the months of illness added up, and my capacity for giving was drying up, love kept showing up. Friends and family arranged rides to appointments, and there was a schedule for people to sign up for sleepover shifts when the side effects were worst and day shifts to help with laundry, chores, and bathing. Meals were delivered, mostly helping to nourish my revolving door of caregivers. Two of my closest friends wrote a letter to my community to raise money to help pay for complementary treatments and hospital costs that my health insurance did not cover. I now had undeniable needs and no bandwidth to refuse help. Dependent on others for the first time in my adult life, I finally had no ability to resist other people's giving. It was clear that my life was going to rely on their kindness and care. I therefore had to face and deepen my own capacity for receiving. As I was cracked open, the love was able to pour in.

Some old friends reemerged and made clear that they had always been uncomfortable with the lack of balance in our relationship and now welcomed the opportunity to help me. Yanked out of my self-protective patterns, I was able to note how important it was for them to have circumstances in which *they* could give and feel appreciated. I was forced to recognize and trust that others could be genuinely filled up by extending generosity and having it received.

Being brought to my knees and unable to give taught me one of the biggest lessons of my life: giving at the expense of receiving is selfish. For all of my earlier focus on supposedly meeting the needs of others, I was actually controlling and hogging all the goodies — depriving the very people I love of the gratification that comes from being generous, and then being on the receiving end of gratitude. I had hijacked the reciprocity cycle. It turned out that the biggest gift I could offer was allowing others to be in a giving position, too. I found a new form of giving — and a new level of gratitude — in the power and vulnerability of receiving.

THE GIFTS OF RELATIONSHIP

Love is blind, we say, but in a deeper sense love is the great eye-opener.
— Brother David Steindl-Rast

We all exist in concentric circles of relationship — some distant and others close, some with people different from us and others with people similar. Some of our circles are given to us; some we create. Living within this intricate web brings us the most extravagant joys and our most excruciating sorrows. Much of how we show up for relationships in our day-to-day lives is running on old, buried wiring systems, so we can end up feeling perpetually at the mercy of others, befuddled by the fact that our efforts toward connection often fizzle or do not light up at all.

The domain of relationships always offers fertile ground for learning. When any two individual forces meet, new energies are created and possibilities forged. New life is born, losses are suffered, love is made holy. We are over and again made both humble and proud. Secure and insecure. Flattered and flattened. Hurt and healed. Relationships deliver our most unbridled magnificence and messiness. And they support our capacity to grow — whether we welcome it in the moment or not.

Strengthening presence, perspective, and possibility in our relationships transforms our experience of interconnectedness and therefore life itself. The future of our species and planet depends on our ability to extend kindness and compassion to others and to cooperate for the vitality of the common good. Recognizing that we are in relationship with our larger human family and our Earth in every moment, we must consider relationships in their most inclusive arc.

Grateful living helps us unleash our most generous selves as we practice taking nothing and no one for granted. We open our hearts to others in ways that open doors and break down barriers. We do not hold back on our desire to show and share affection. We respond rather than react, inquire rather than judge. In this awakened field of compassion and generosity, our relationships become the terrain for the practice of living gratefully, nourishing and transforming us and others.

BECOME PRESENT TO YOUR CONNECTEDNESS

Love isn't a feeling, it is a practice. — Erich Fromm

Our relationships are powerful portals to the fullness of life. The moments when we have a real connection with another human being can deliver us into a profound feeling of communion. But these experiences of communion are infrequent, as we often reserve our fullest presence for a select few. Grateful living invites us to expand our practice of wholehearted presence into larger circles of connection.

Gratefulness reminds us that we are held in the world's wide and gracious embrace, and we should consider and appreciate the gifts of this vast web of relatedness. We must consistently open our awareness to the countless ways in which we already belong to each other, the ways that we are already reliant, supported, and interdependent:

> **Gratefully recognize** the people on whom you rely simply to be kept alive, to be well, and to enjoy basic comforts: those who deliver your mail, build roads, make clothing, grow food, develop medicine, and provide you with millions of other gifts of love and labor.

> **Thankfully affirm** the lineage of which you are the manifestation in this moment. This web extends back in time to embrace all the ancestors who made sacrifices, made choices, and made love in order that you would be here now. This web extends forward through generations that will come after you, impacted by every choice made and not made by our global collective.

> **Appreciatively acknowledge** the constellation of ties you have with the people in your life — friends, family, coworkers, community. Whether or not you are actively in touch with all of these people, they hold you and you hold them. They have made you who you are and you have helped to make them. These relational networks are some of the greatest sources of meaning that we experience, and they warrant being held with our most humble and generous regard.

Appreciative Presence

Typically, when we think of being more grateful in our relationships, we focus on expressing gratitude for the things that people do for us or give to us — the unexpected kindness, the gesture of support, the thoughtful gift, the fabulous meal. Getting better at offering this kind of gratitude is a worthy aspiration; reciprocity is a mighty energy exchange. Whenever we do express thanks — the more specific, personal, sincere, and creative we can be is what will make the gesture most meaningful for those we seek to acknowledge.

Yet thanking people for what they do for us is only a small dose of the healing medicine that our appreciation can offer. A grateful orientation invites us to focus on appreciating people without them having done any-thing to benefit us directly. To cultivate a deeper recognition of gratitude for someone's existence — not for something tangible they have done or given — is a different focus. While this may seem a slight distinction, it is actually a significant difference in approach — one that is not transactional but grounded in poignancy and vulnerability. We recognize that the people in our lives are true gifts, impacting us in large and small ways. We understand their presence as a blessing that could be otherwise, and someday will be.

Sharing appreciation for others from gratefulness rather than simple gratitude allows us to more fully celebrate the exquisite existence of the peo-ple in our midst. In this way, we open our hearts to see and acknowledge our vulnerable ties of interconnection. When we seek to express forms of appreci-ation that transcend gratitude based on what we are "getting," the sentiments will sound and feel different as they are offered and received:

> **Acknowledge** that people have endless options about how they can share their time and hearts. No matter the relationship, choice is involved — and the choice is either re-upped or not. Try acknowledging this fact with words: "I am grateful you are in my life." Or, "I am so grateful you choose to be with me today."

> **Recognize** that people are distinct from you, individuated in a constant process of becoming themselves. Being seen and accepted as a distinct human being matters a lot in rela-tionships, not simply being appreciated for how we benefit

one another. Recognizing that another person is a unique, ever-changing human, you could say, "I am grateful for who you are." Or, simply, "I appreciate you."

Affirm people and help them know that they are seen for how they move through the larger world, not just how they impact you. Focus on the specific attributes of someone. With an eye toward particulars, you could say something like "I am so grateful for how kindly you treat strangers, the creativity you bring to your work, the integrity of your choices, the ripples of joy you leave in your wake."

✳

When you recognize the true gifts and opportunities of relationship, with whom do you feel moved to connect? What are some things you might say to offer meaningful appreciation?

✳

What are some habits, patterns, or beliefs that steal your capacity to be fully present in your relationships? What commitments can you make to increase your availability?

VOICES OF GRATEFUL LIVING

I recently found myself in a self-critical spiral. It was pretty strong and suffocating. But somehow a couple of conversations I had with people, and a reflection on how that spiral came about, nudged me to look from the perspective of what I had done that was good. My accomplishments, the people whose lives I had affected and who had affected mine. I wrote it all down and looked over these truths of my life. This noticing has helped me in the days since to know that opportunities exist now and, in the future, to find and create joy. Life is a mixed bag. We live, we learn, we grow. We have been, but we are also becoming. — Denise L.

SEEK A PERSPECTIVE OF HUMILITY AND GENEROSITY

Love has come to rule and transform. Stay awake, my heart, stay awake. — Rumi

Gratefulness is the opposite of taking life — and the human family that belongs to life — for granted. When we take people for granted, we have stopped listening to them, operating on the assumption that there is nothing more to understand, nothing they can teach us, no way they could move or bless us, or crack us open. The gifts that both strangers and those intimate to us are bearing become invisible. We forget to wonder how any of the little things that happen in someone's day could make them a different person from the one who woke up this morning. We forget to inquire about the kindness they experienced, the hurts they may have been soothing all afternoon, and the joys that may have made their heart beat quicker. We miss their changes, and we miss being changed by them. To take people for granted is to make them inanimate — a dusty book on the shelf that we read once and then walk by every day without seeing, or one we never even bothered to crack open. Too often we assume that we know the story line of people and books by heart. Yet is is said we are never the same person after reading even one page of a book.

We all know the feeling of being taken for granted, the feeling that what we offer is expected and unvalued. This experience can generate a loneliness and longing that being physically alone never incites. We may be with some- one, or a group of people, and feel invisible. What we long for is acknowl- edgment and appreciation of our presence — to know our existence and our offerings matter. And while we can't guarantee that this recognition comes to us from others, we can offer it. Living gratefully reminds us — and others — that we are alive, that we are here, and that we matter.

The feeling of being taken for granted is often healed by curiosity. Our ability to be truly inquisitive is a direct reflection of our capacity for generos- ity and humility. Curiosity turns our whole selves toward what is unknown. It establishes our vulnerability and interest in learning. Listening affirms the inherent worth in others, and in life itself. When we neglect to live from a place of curiosity, we send a message that we feel complete as we are and would rather recycle stale information than explore and let ourselves be impacted by new understanding — so much of which is awakened in our connections. Not opening up to deeply listen to others is an attempt to close ourselves off from the rawness of humility and vulnerability. The costs of not listening are high. The highest price we pay is real love.

When you listen from a grateful perspective, you embody graciousness. You have the intention to listen and learn, and to love. There are so many ways to expand connection and to have experiences with others that leave all parties more grateful, especially when circumstances are challenging.

The starting place for any generous interchange is humility — the ability to admit not knowing, the willingness to be wrong, the capacity to admit our weaknesses, wounds, and imperfections and not feel mortally flawed or fall apart. If we pay attention, we will see that those people who have a hard time being humble will not admit their mistakes and will be challenged to say, "I am sorry." These same people will likely also have a hard time saying, "I am grateful," or even "Thank you." If someone struggles with apologizing, it is likely also challenging for them to express appreciation. Both arise from a space of vulnerability, consideration, and accountability, which are necessary ingredients in any conscious relationship. They are also key qualities of gratefulness, necessary in the healing of our connections, and therefore our ability to transform our world.

✻

Understanding inquiry as a form of generosity, what are some
questions that help others know you are truly interested?

✻

How do you embody humility in your relationships? Seeing humility
as a form of generosity, how could you embody it even more?

AWAKEN THE POSSIBILITY OF DEEPER CONNECTIONS

We are born in relationship, we are wounded in relationship, and we can be healed in relationship. — Harville Hendrix

Many of us were taught the Golden Rule: *Do unto others as you would have them do unto you.* This maxim was often dictated by parents or teachers who sought to corral selfish behavior in children, and to inspire their generosity and gratitude.

But the Golden Rule is tricky. It assumes our needs and longings are universal and that everyone around us shares our desires for how they want to be treated. Of course, it won't hurt to follow the Golden Rule — focusing on offering more of the appreciation and respect we want can be a good thing — but assuming sameness and doing to others what we want done to us is no assurance of golden relationships. It could actually make them leaden.

The Golden Rule can become the "Grateful Rule" if we turn it around to say: Do unto others as *they* would have you do unto *them*. This now becomes an exercise in tuning in to another person with care and curiosity rather than projecting our own needs and desires on people. If we give others what *we* want, we not only miss the chance for meaningful connection but also repeatedly try to make others feel our care and never hit *their* mark — never awaken possibility for them. Never touch their heart. And never give rise to the truly grateful feelings that nurture our connections.

Instead, we can recognize the interesting differences between us. Each human being we encounter has a profoundly distinct history that shaped who they are and what matters and is meaningful to them, especially people who come from backgrounds very different from ours. The things that bring a sense of hurt and invisibility, or love and possibility, are simply not the same for everyone. Welcome this awareness of difference rather than resting in the reassurances of sameness.

If we want to offer genuine care, we must be willing to ask generative questions, such as "What matters most to you?" or "What do you need right now?" And then listen very attentively. In asking these kinds of illuminating questions, we lean in. We literally turn toward the other person without an agenda and move our hearts closer, softened to receive. We listen not only with our ears but by attuning ourselves completely to the presence of the other person in all of their mystery and magic. We put down our projections so as to be available to whatever emerges. Not only are we sitting in front of someone who is different from us, but in a thousand small ways they are not even the same person they were yesterday. In not taking someone for granted, we invite them to continually show up, changed. This is hallowed territory. And it is a profound blessing when someone offers themselves this way.

There are so many possibilities to transform our relationships if we are willing to stay curious, admit how little we know, and how much there is to learn. We do not need to have all the answers, but we have to truly want closeness in order to experience and unleash the blessings of connection. It is making these kinds of meaningful connections, especially to love and learn from people who are different from us, which will help bring needed healing to our lives and world.

We become agents of change when we allow our hearts to open and inquire. But grateful living only leads to healing if we respond based on what we hear. We need to demonstrate through words and actions that we hold what we learn from and about others as sacred. It is what we say and do with this information that will awaken all the possibilities of love.

✴

In what relationships could you generate a deeper connection by practicing the Grateful Rule instead of the Golden Rule?

✴

How can you stretch yourself with more generosity toward people you have been anxious about connecting with?

VOICES OF GRATEFUL LIVING

At one time in my life I might have thought gratitude was insincere mushy stuff, but I have learned better. The gifts of each moment, like the soft pine needles I just walked on with my dog, the lights of hope in neighbors' windows, and the memories of those who have loved me, are worth celebrating. Gratitude can surge up through tears of joy if we let it. It's in the nonverbal grace of: "You belong here" when we enter a room, unsure. It's in the tap dance of a beloved dog when we return after a short absence, in the eyes of a baby who trusts us. Gratitude is not insincere words or a phony "thank you for your time" when we'd like to say something else. It is the force that will make our words resonate, our lives radiant, and our world capable of reconciliation — if we let it. — Maria S.

DARN LUCKY

It happens, you know — the day opens itself
like a tulip in a warm room, and you meet someone
who amazes you with their willingness
to be a thousand percent alive, someone
who makes you feel grateful to be you.
And it's as if life has been keeping a beautiful
secret from you — like the fact that they make
elderberry flowers into wine. Like muscadine.
Like the yellow-green floral scent of quince.
Like the perfect knot for tying your shoes.
And it turns out life does have wonderful
secrets waiting for you. Even when the news
makes you cry. Even when some old pain returns,
that's when you will meet this new friend.
Someone wholly themselves. Someone
who makes you smile in the kitchen, a smile so real
that when you go out, the whole world notices.
It's enough to make you want to wake up in the morning.
To go into the day. To be unguarded as a tulip, petals
falling open. You never know who you might meet.
— Rosemerry Wahtola Trommer

GRATEFUL FOR EACH MOMENT

Sometimes our light goes out but is blown again into instant flame by an
encounter with another human being. Each of us owes the deepest thanks
to those who have rekindled this inner light. — Albert Schweitzer

We are all held in many forms of relationships, and we also hold countless
relationships in our hands and hearts. It is in these webs of connection that
we are made and remade through each of our encounters — some lasting a
lifetime, others a mere moment. Sometimes we are the maker, sometimes we
are made, sometimes both. Always, we can be touched and transformed.

Grateful living helps us to not take our relationships for granted, to become more awake to the magnificence of people, and to better recognize their gifts and needs. We become better able to offer full-on presence, a reverent perspective, and real responsiveness. In the unpredictable terrain of relationships, when we endeavor to connect gratefully with others, we open to what it means to be fully human. Showing up wholeheartedly always affirms the values of love, vulnerability, and courage of the heart — the impact of which extends far beyond the connections that enrich our daily lives. These are the qualities for which the world is longing.

※

May you hold your relationships as sacred, with humility and generosity.

Practices and Prompts

STOP. LOOK. GO. PRACTICE
The Grateful Rule in Challenging Conversations

It is a powerful practice to ask someone for a reparative conversation. It is when we show up fully for challenging times in our relationships that true care is awakened and established. It is always worthwhile to initiate a healing connection — these are the moments when humility and courage are indistinguishable. The Grateful Rule can help us lean in and learn from challenging dynamics and conversations: "Do unto others as they would have you do unto them." Ultimately, whatever we learn must be acknowledged, appreciated, and acted upon if it is to have a positive effect on the relationship and on us. This is where we have the opportunity to "walk our talk."

> **Stop:** Cultivate a soft and strong presence to the situation in which you find yourself connected with another person. Notice how you feel in your body when relationship dynamics become challenging. Anchor yourself in your breath. Notice how your mind may jump ahead to anticipate where the conversation may lead. Bring your thoughts fully into the present moment.

Notice how your heart and feelings may be tender and anxious. Welcome whatever emotions arise with compassion. Deepen your trust and courage with your breath.

Look: Recognize the opportunities that this connection is making available to you. Acknowledge the gift of connecting with this particular person. It may be difficult, but even with a conversation that feels challenging, try to reframe the experience from obligation to opportunity: "I get to listen as a way of showing care. I get to grow and learn." Whatever the case, look for the opportunity to show up wholeheartedly, and in doing so, to cultivate a sense of mutual belonging. Embrace the poignancy of the moment and the potential that it holds.

Go: Start by sharing appreciation for any of the opportunities that you see this connection offering you. Be specific. Get yourself grounded in being grateful for this opportunity. It sets a hopeful, helpful tone. Next, release your assumptions and projections. Open yourself fully to learn from this conversation. Explore some open, curious, Grateful Rule kinds of questions. Lean in and listen: What do you want me to be sure to understand? What would make you feel seen and understood right now? What could I do or say that would be reparative or healing for you? What would be meaningful to you as an outcome of this conversation? What other questions would help get to the heart of the matter at hand?

No matter how the conversation goes, be sure to express appreciation for the other person's presence and participation before you part. It can be helpful to make a gesture or commitment that lets the other person know they have been heard. Speak in ways that reflect what you have learned. It is always good to share humble learning and appreciation. It offers reinforcement to a tender heart — yours and the other's.

Listen with Presence

When you are engaged in an interaction, you might believe you are fully present, but the repeated invitation to drop in a little deeper can take you to unexpected levels. Take a breath or two to be more wholly available. Purposefully release thoughts not related to the interaction and notice what becomes accessible when you bring all your attention to the moment. Experiment with holding eye contact and notice how you can listen with your eyes as well as your ears. Tune in to what is being said, and really *hear* it. Let yourself be impacted by what you hear. Listen to listen. Invite your heart to become more grateful. Notice the abundance of relatedness that arises. If you find yourself distracted, invite yourself to come back into appreciative presence. Keep dropping deeper. It works wonders. You might even experiment with using this presence-practice with someone you are meeting for the first time and notice what unfolds in your connection.

Three-Word Wonders

"I love you" is a potent gift if offered with sincerity. So are many other words. Experiment with generating or deepening a conversation with just three words. Begin practicing with them and witness what happens. Write them down to remind yourself. Try these to offer the gifts of your humility and generosity to others.

> Appreciation: I am grateful . . .
> Recognition: I can see . . .
> Curiosity: I am wondering . . .
> Inquiry: Help me understand . . .
> Presence: I am here . . .
> Validation: It makes sense . . .
> Empathy: I can imagine . . .
> Humility: I am sorry . . .
> Wisdom: Let's pause briefly . . .

Gratefulize

Regularly letting people know that we notice them and they matter makes a huge difference — and it is highly contagious. It costs us nothing and has the potential to change everything. It is hard to get this one wrong if your grateful heart leads the way.

Make a list of people you tend to take for granted, or who have changed your life for the better and you never really let them know. Think of your many circles of connection — family, friends, colleagues, neighbors, acquaintances. Each day, choose at least one person to "gratefulize" in whatever way you are moved to do so — it could be through a note, an email, an e-card, a phone call, or a gesture of kindness in person. Make this a daily practice, and be as generous and specific with each person as you can be. Revel in the ripple effects.

PERSPECTIVE PROMPTS
Reduce Your Chances for Regret

Every time you embrace poignancy in a relationship, you reduce the chance for regret. Living as though nothing is promised, you cultivate the ability to be fully present with your vulnerability and therefore with others. Being able to harness the opportunities in a given moment of connection is powerful. You can recognize the ever-present possibility that such moments may not come again, and so make them truly matter. Show up with your heart open, knowing that it costs you nothing and affords you everything.

Think about the ways that you greet or say goodbye to people — each one is an opening for meaning-making. Make eye contact. Hug like it matters — it does. Say something meaningful and sincere. Take the time to make a real connection. Make it last. You will never regret it.

✴

Every greeting and goodbye offers me the chance to show love and appreciation.

Welcome Distance

Carl Sagan astutely said, "For small creatures such as we, the vastness is bearable only through love." The wider we turn the aperture on the lens through which we see our lives, and the more distance we have, the closer we can feel. Love becomes more meaningful when held against a vast backdrop. Our experience of belonging expands as we gain peak awareness, and we can see the relationships for which we are grateful in a longer arc of time and space. Perspective allows us to better see the positive difference we make for others as well.

Consider the people who have impacted you positively, whether for a fleeting moment or a lifetime. Know and trust this same place you have held in the lives of others.

✳

The love in my life holds me close, especially when the world feels vast and unwieldy.

Relationships Are Choices

The relationships in our lives are gifts, not guarantees. We all may be lovable, but having truly loving relationships is a privilege. Relationships reflect the choices people make again and again to show up and share a part of life with us. To be chosen is a blessing. And our relationships deserve to be honored and tended as choices, not givens, no matter how many or few we have. The more we can experience the extraordinary nature of what it takes to establish and maintain connections over time, the more grateful we will be, and the more gracious love will be with us.

Allow people to know how blessed you feel by their choice to sustain a connection with you. Experience love as a privilege and appreciate the plentiful ways it offers itself up in your life.

✳

Relationships are a blessing and I treasure the many ways they show up as love in my life.

Give Close Attention to What You Hold Dear

It's easy to espouse a long list of core values and beliefs about how a relationship *should* be. It is easy to come up with ideas about the characteristics of a healthy relationship — reciprocity and mutuality, respect and vulnerability, gentleness and generosity. But how often are you actually practicing and giving your closest attention to what you hold most dear? Allow your principles to truly guide you in how to engage in your relationships most gratefully; you will readily reap the benefits.

Take some time to reconnect with your core values about what it takes to sustain healthy relationships and let these commitments guide how you tend your choices in connection.

＊

My values offer me trustworthy guidance in nurturing connections
I am grateful for.

Share Joy

Our connections open us to meaning and delight. Play, laughter, dancing, and singing can all be so much richer when shared. Connecting with others multiplies the things that we love most in life and adds to our shared memories. There is such pleasure in opening our senses with another human being — holding someone's hand, savoring a meal, beholding a canopy of stars or a sunrise, listening to music. No matter how much we revel in time alone, sharing experiences with others shapes many of our most grateful moments in life.

Think of shared experiences that have awakened you to greater joy and brought enjoyment to others. Initiate more occasions that will make you and others grateful for the opportunity to share life.

＊

Sharing my sources of delight and enjoyment makes for a
more grateful life.

CHAPTER 9

HOLDING THE HEART OF GRIEF AND LOSS

On Wings and Prayers

I cannot say for sure that my first conversation with God was actually *with* God, but I knew I was aiming my plea at a sacred space above my body and bed, above my room and the roof over my head, above the dim lights of town, and up into the ether and the enveloping stars. I was in a solicitous frame of mind, and I needed an opportunity to feel connected to something gracious and boundless.

My plea went something like this: *Okay. If it is truly necessary to die at this age, I will. But please let my death have as much meaning as my life could have had if I had been able to live longer. And if I live, please let my life have as much meaning as an early death could have had.*

I did not expect this prayer to come out of me. I did not want to die. I had purposeful work, friends and family I cherished, and endless ways that I loved to fritter and focus my time. I had been meditating, doing yoga, taking supplements, and eating organic food well before these things became mainstream. I loved life and had always felt heartily attached to it — the longer the better as far as I was concerned. My petition to the universe alerted me that things were shifting.

It was becoming clear that if quantity of life could not be promised to me, perhaps there could be greater promise in both living and dying consciously, and without so many conditions. I knew quite a bit about loving unconditionally, but I had never really entertained the idea of living unconditionally — without attachment to where it was all going, or for how long. Well-known wisdom advised me, "Be here now" and "Live each day as if it were your last." While this wisdom was worthy of pondering, it seemed better suited to book titles, and much harder to try to live by.

Long before being given an "end-stage" diagnosis, I had been moved by stories of extraordinary young people whose lives had been cut short by terminal diseases. I found myself seeking out their timeless wisdom. When I listened to teenagers and young adults reckon with dire prognoses, I was awestruck by their perspective, wished our world had more of it, and wondered if I could live with such courage and clarity. The fact that their lives would be cut short seemed less important to them than living such that their loved ones knew that *they* knew each day mattered. They had the lucidity I craved: to act on what I knew was important, including wearing my heart on my sleeve, speaking my truth, showing up fully for life, exhibiting love unabashedly, making every moment count. They had given themselves permission to hold nothing back, and this inspired me to know what I wanted my first real prayer to be, whenever the time came.

The time had come. Chemotherapy was taking a toll, and not just because of the side effects.

My spinal fusion was not enduring the chemo well; it seemed to be unfusing, leaving me more compromised and in more pain than palliative medication could touch. I had no idea whether the cancer was retreating, but according to the doctors, I had to carry on with the daily injections and keep to my treatment schedule regardless. That summer, I wrote in a letter to friends and family: "The cancer and the chemo are doing vicious battle over my body. I have no idea who is going to win, but they won't get my spirit. Of that, even in the worst of times, I feel sure."

This idea that there was something more to me than what was limited by my body and mind was a rather new concept. Imagining I was held within a spirit that could transcend the battles being waged in the physical realm brought me great relief. It also gave substance to my prayer that if I did not get to live as long as I wanted, I could pack my remaining moments with meaning and live on in the hearts of those who loved me, as well as in some larger ethereal embodiment. This was a great comfort during my most difficult hours.

It was also a comfort to me because, for the first time, I was experiencing losses. People I had befriended during my illness and treatment were dying, including those with less advanced or aggressive diagnoses than mine. During my treatment, I went to the memorial services for two members of my women's cancer support group, and then a funeral for the leader herself. These were women doing everything right, everything they could, everything they were reassured would make a positive difference in their odds for survival. I struggled to reconcile my own continuation; at times I could not help but think it should have been me succumbing, not them. And becoming closer to death through facing theirs made the possibility of my death seem like it was lurking ever nearer.

As I gained deeper insight and ease about the prospect of my own death, it helped me better cope with the losses around me. If I was convinced that my life could be measured in meaningful moments and memories more than simply years, and that the love I had shared while I was alive would endure, I absolutely had to imagine that this could be possible for others who were dying as well. Impossibly heartbreaking as each loss was, I felt there was something I could offer: I could assure people that I would allow the meaning of their lives and deaths to grow in my broken heart, through me, and out into the world.

In promising this, I was able to fulfill both parts of my prayer at once — making loss and life more meaningful, without condition. I could say to those I loved and lost the one thing I had to offer, the one thing I longed to feel as true in my own grieving heart and know would be enough: *I will not take your life or loss for granted. Your legacy will live on in me. In your honor, I will acknowledge and celebrate the gift of every moment with a grateful heart.*

ON BEING INTIMATE WITH LIFE AND LOSS

It isn't primarily a practice of thinking of one's last hour, or of death as a physical phenomenon; it is a seeing of every moment of life against the horizon of death, and a challenge to incorporate that awareness of dying into every moment so as to become more fully alive. — Brother David Steindl-Rast

It is one of life's greatest paradoxes: The more we welcome the assuredness of our own mortality and the transience of all that we hold dear, the more fully alive we can become. The more fully alive we become, the more present we will be to our losses. In acknowledging the finite nature of everything tangible, we open ourselves such that everyone and every moment can matter. This eyes-wide-open path is forged in the depths of our hearts and will take us into the woods of love and loss, requiring vulnerability, courage, and faith as we make our way. Gratefully, it is a journey that will offer us immeasurable blessings and unexpected gifts in return.

The measure of our grief is a testimony to our capacity to love. As civil rights activist Valarie Kaur so aptly says, "Joy is the gift of love. Grief is the cost of love." We most often associate the depths of grief with the deeply felt personal loss of a loved one. But grief is also felt with the loss of a beloved animal, job, home, community, or physical ability. Grief is the cost of loving and respecting life, our Earth and all its inhabitants, and our values of fairness, safety, justice, love, and dignity. We suffer empathetic grief when we know others suffer. We suffer collective grief when there is suffering in the world. The more we love, the more we courageously commit to walking through life thin-skinned, bound to the full range of how much the heart can feel, break, and break itself open — ultimately into even greater wholeness. It is the acceptance and courageous trust we muster every moment of our uncertain lives that carry us inward and onward with peace.

Whether our hearts are heavy with the loss of someone important, the loss of aspects of our own lives, or the losses we feel in and for the world, it can be challenging to feel gratitude, but gratefulness is itself a sanctuary. Gratitude and grief walk hand in hand, reminding us it is precisely those things we treasure most that open us to the pain of loss, and bring healing to this terrain. Living gratefully, we recognize that we are offered no guarantees in life, and there is little that we can count on besides this very moment. But this moment is the most significant gift we have, and to live and love fully in the face of the inevitability of loss is to shape a life worthy of our big hearts.

BECOME PRESENT TO IMPERMANENCE

Impermanence is a principle of harmony. When we don't struggle against it, we are in harmony with reality. — Pema Chödrön

Over and over we must lean into the truth of impermanence and feel ourselves made more whole in the weight of its certainty. Getting comfortable with impermanence allows us to more deeply appreciate all the things we do not want to take for granted — our body, emotions, relationships, and mystery. There are few things more certain than the fact that we will experience change and loss in many aspects of our lives and, ultimately, loss of our own life. We cannot fool the heart — it knows that love, loss, and longing come from the same source. This awareness is the wide-open doorway to poignancy and treasuring life as a gift.

Our ability to treasure life and love is what promises us heartbreak, and our ability to hold heartbreak is what promises us love and life to treasure. It is in the exact moments that we feel most alive that we are aware of both the beauty and pain of life's transience. We must commit ourselves to grief as one of life's essential elements. To live with the illusion that we can protect ourselves from loss is to sleepwalk through our days, and we pay the price in our capacity for presence. The inevitability of loss is not just a wake-up call; it is a bell ringing at regular intervals to remind us of what matters.

The truth of impermanence invites us to be intimate with immediacy as we come to feel the weight of this moment as the only place where we can truly be alive. This aliveness commits us to feeling everything more fully: grief and gratitude, pain and pleasure. In moments of sorrow, we remember that grief is only awakened by the loss of something we have cherished. Gratefulness holds us, and the entirety of our experience, within this truth.

✳

How could you more fully notice and welcome the truth of impermanence in your day-to-day life, knowing that it may actually offer greater peace?

✳

What are a few things you have had to lose or let go of in order to gain what you now treasure? What can this awareness help you accept and keep in mind for future losses?

VOICES OF GRATEFUL LIVING

When going through one of the hardest times in my life, I was introduced to the practice of gratitude. I thought it was ridiculous to find anything to be grateful for as I mourned the loss of my twin babies. But, one day, I began. Slowly, I realized that while I had lost much, I had also gained much. I saw the abundance in my life — the love, support, delicious foods, cozy blankets, soft cats, sunshine. Practicing changed me. Gratefulness has kept me on track with my daily practice for years, and it's supported me in having a mind-set of gratitude and positivity that has become fundamental to who I am as a human. — Kristine S.

SEEK A PERSPECTIVE OF ACCEPTANCE AND COURAGE

The only choice we have as we mature is how we inhabit our vulnerability, how we become larger and more courageous and more compassionate through our intimacy with disappearance. — David Whyte

Impermanence will undoubtedly, significantly impact our lives — and its attendant grief will deliver sorrow to our hearts in both expected and unexpected ways. We are all vulnerable to grief's arrival, and none of us can predict it or protect ourselves from it, nor should we try. To do so would require living with a hypervigilant or hardened heart. As tempting as it is to try to shield ourselves from the pain of heartache, it is precisely the heart's aliveness that allows us to feel broken and open. Grief reminds us that we can allow for other forms of deep feeling to surface, too, if we can soften to the invitation. The doorway of grief is connected to the doorway of empathy and joy.

There are many forms of loss, and one is not like any other. Though each experience is singular, loss connects us to each other and to our human family in fundamental ways. Surviving any one loss does not make suffering additional losses easier, or more difficult. Each is an experience unto itself, unimaginable, unforgettable, and it can come — with the balm of time — to be better understood for its teachings. Life promises us few things but change as a constant. And loss as a form of change will come unbeckoned into each of our lives, in both daily and more dramatic ways.

With the blessing and burden of our bodies, we notice that we are changing and growing older every day. This is an often disconcerting reality of our incarnation, as well as a natural and beautiful one. When we approach aging as a form of small, daily blessings and gifts, losses and grievances, it can provide a useful terrain of practice for building a reservoir of gratefulness in the face of all that is unpredictable. In embracing the gift of aging, it helps to recognize that one day even this gift will go away.

Growing older, with all its upsides and downsides, is the only way we get the privilege of remaining alive. Aging opens us to surprise, both heartening and disheartening — not one without the other. We open ourselves to new ways of seeing and being ourselves and new ways of seeing and being with others. We have experiences of both grace and grief, and we develop courage to help us welcome whatever comes.

Love offers a similar paradox of abundant gifts and inevitable loss. When we commit to loving, we commit to losing, because in love we attach ourselves to someone we will ultimately be required to let go — by either the loss of our life or theirs. Our commitment to staying present for loss is also the commitment to stay connected with love. They are interwoven, so to cut our hearts off from one is to cut us off from both. Loss happens, and there is no cure for it other than to grieve and love all the more. And in honoring our grief, grateful living calls on us to honor the love and gratitude that inspired it.

✳

How has your experience of aging taught you the courage of vulnerability? How might this courage serve you in times of grief?

✳

When you accept something — even if it does not feel easy or acceptable — how does this help you better learn from it?

AWAKEN POSSIBILITY IN LOSS

*If grief can be a doorway to love, then let us all weep for the world
we are breaking apart so we can love it back to wholeness again.*
— Thich Nhat Hanh

It is said that loss is often what teaches us about the value of things. If this is true, then gratefulness would like to arrive into our lives well before loss knocks on the door. While loss will surely still visit, living each day gratefully offers a more gracious and generative way to be in touch with how much love we have for things and people *before* they are gone.

There is nothing we can do about the inevitability of loss, but there is a huge amount we can do about not losing ourselves and those things that matter to us when we are alive, even while grieving. The invitation is to connect with our hearts fully every day so we can look back with as little regret as possible, knowing we have been in touch with — and unabashedly shared — our appreciation for everything that has brought our life meaning. Living gratefully offers us this pathway, and the small price we pay is the vulnerability of wearing our hearts and passions on our sleeves. It is worth everything it costs.

Scholar and activist Joanna Macy says, "We need pain to alert us for what needs attention." Living with poignancy wakes us up, allowing grief to be as accessible and acceptable as wonder or joy. Poignancy makes it so that our grief is not felt as a betrayal to joy, and our joy is not experienced as a betrayal to grief. Gratefulness holds everything at once, knowing that all our emotional experiences belong within the same heart-embrace. Doing our best to accept what unfolds, we trust that all of our biggest emotions arrive with lessons if we do not resist their form.

When something or someone dies, some amount of possibility is lost, and this loss informs our grief. The future we had envisioned is no longer an option. However, new possibilities are also awakened. Our invitation is to discover possibility in the midst of our losses. What is emerging to take the place of what is gone? What opens in that void? What new kindnesses does loss allow? It is a brave heart that can consider these questions and more fully welcome occasions of change.

We often experience grief as private and solitary, but loss is a collective and unifying reality. We discover possibility when we hold our anguish in the space of the commons. In that openness, we open others to their pain as we can help others open to the full landscape of their hurt, and from the truth of that shared experience, the possibility of more love and more beauty emerges for everyone. Shutting our grief away denies the relational nature of our hearts and cuts us off from healing, because grief is a doorway to understanding what we value and cherish.

The more open and courageous we can be about feeling and sharing our grief, the more deeply we will make meaning from our experiences of loss. Simultaneously brokenhearted and wholehearted, we long to tell our stories, share our courage and our hurt. The world needs the cocreation of rituals, ceremony, and truth-telling that will heal our collective heart.

We are waiting for one another, waiting to be met with the gaze that says, "I know. Let's heal together." Make an effort to offer the gaze you are longing for. The world is waiting for people who can hold the profound truth of love, gratitude, and grief simultaneously.

※

What can you notice about the kindness and thoughtfulness that
often arise in the face of grief?

※

How does grief open you to feel more connected to others?
What could you do to make grief a less isolating experience?

VOICES OF GRATEFUL LIVING

We recently lost our 32-year-old son to leukemia. Practicing gratitude for his life and the time we shared brings comfort, soothes the pain, and helps us cope with staggering grief and loss. Of course, our compassion and empathy toward others who suffer has grown. — Doug V.

THE UNBROKEN

There is a brokenness
out of which comes the unbroken,
a shatteredness
out of which blooms the unshatterable.
There is a sorrow
beyond all grief which leads to joy
and a fragility
out of whose depths emerges strength.

There is a hollow space
too vast for words
through which we pass with each loss,
out of whose darkness
we are sanctioned into being.

There is a cry deeper than all sound
whose serrated edges cut the heart
as we break open to the place inside
which is unbreakable and whole,
while learning to sing.
— Rashani Réa

GRATEFUL FOR EACH MOMENT

Someone I loved once gave me a box full of darkness.
It took me years to understand that this too, was a gift.
— Mary Oliver

Saint Benedict said that in order to become more alive, you must "keep death always before your eyes." This was a key source of inspiration in Brother David's decision to devote himself to monastic life. How is it that such a challenging proclamation could rouse a longing to study and serve? How could it possibly make us more grateful? Impermanence is a powerful invitation because it resonates with a recognized truth about life: we know that loss and grief will accompany us forever and will be there to bid us farewell, so we will be well-served to wake up to their teachings now.

Grateful living offers a place to sink safely into the truth of your tender heart. May it offer a harbor where you feel comforted in your unique losses and also reminded of your connection to your larger human family. May gratefulness be a sanctuary where grief and gratitude hold one another in close communion, and where you are reminded that you are always at home.

※

May you hold the losses and grief in your life with acceptance and courage.

Practices and Prompts

STOP. LOOK. GO. PRACTICE
Blessing for the Loss of a Loved One
Sometimes in life we face the blessing and burden of knowing in advance that someone we love will die. Anticipating and accepting the loss of a loved one can be incredibly sorrowful. It can also present a powerful opportunity to let that person know what they mean to you.

> **Stop:** Take some long, slow breaths with the intention to breathe in sorrow and exhale peace. Breathe the softness of sorrow into your lungs and lower belly, and then into your heart. Hold your breath for a long moment, and then exhale the peace of presence until your belly feels soft. Repeat until you feel peacefulness.

> **Look:** Notice the feelings in your heart right now. Let yourself recognize their weight. Feel both the palpable presence and absence of what and whom you love. Hold this love close.

> **Go:** Write a letter to the person you love with the specific intent to offer healing by letting them know the ways that they have been *enough* simply as they are. It is a gift we can offer to those who are leaving us or have left us when we let them know that they have not let us down. It is also a significant reminder of sufficiency we can offer ourselves. No matter what happens with this letter, allow the ritual of writing it to share your grateful heart.

Here is an excerpt of a letter I wrote to one of my dearest friends in her last weeks of life; though I could not be with her, I sent it to be read aloud to her:

> *Dear P—*
>
> *You are a radiant beam of light that will never go out. You always have been. You will continue to shine and will stay alive forever in all those who love you.*
>
> *Your heart is one of the biggest and best that has ever lived, and it has inspired, touched, and moved so many people. Your heart will carry on. Your love has been extraordinarily generous and kind. It will continue to ripple out in concentric circles forever.*
>
> *You are leaving me and so many others with meaningful memories to hold throughout a lifetime. Thank you. While I cannot help but wish for more time with you, I also want to bless you with the deep assurance that it has been enough. You need not worry. You have been enough. You have been more than enough. You have been pure, abundant blessing in my life and in the lives of so many. Thank you for all of the many gifts — tangible and intangible — that I will have and carry with me forever because of knowing and loving you. I will live my life in your honor and will not let you die to my heart or the world.*

Harvesting Love from Loss

Think of a beloved person whose loss you suffered long enough ago that thinking about their absence does not feel overly acute. With the first person who comes to mind, write a list of ten things that wake up your heart when you think of them — special memories, gifts you received, laughs you shared, meaning that they brought, qualities you cherished. When you are finished, go to the top of the list and write at the front of each item the words, "I am grateful to remember . . ."

Your capacity to have your heart awakened is a gift that can never be taken away. Filling yourself with gratitude now, even if it feels particularly poignant, is an important way of honoring yourself, your connection, and the person you miss. Let your heart ride on a sweet wave of grateful love.

Outreach from the Heart

One of the most challenging things life may deliver is learning about the loss of someone important to us after we have lost touch with them. The heart holds this kind of grief hard, as it can be intermingled with regret and guilt. We have the opportunity in our lives to allow gratefulness to direct us toward making and maintaining contact with the people we care for most.

Keep a list of people with whom you have lost contact but do not want to truly lose. Reach out to at least one person a week and let them know they matter to you, even if you cannot stay in touch as much as you would like. Regardless of whether you hear back, this is a worthwhile effort, a healing balm to your heart and to the hearts of others.

PERSPECTIVE PROMPTS
Embrace Loss Amid the Great Fullness of Life

When you are actively grieving, it is easy to connect with poignancy because it is ever-present. Poignancy helps you remember the preciousness of every moment and the possibility of loss in the midst of daily life. This makes living more honest and vivid, and keeps regrets at a distance. Poignancy also arises when we bring gratefulness for the gift of life into the same space as our sorrow, a paradox that strengthens the heart and leads us forward with the truth of love. Life is a gift. Love is a gift. Loss is only felt in the fullness of life and love.

Hold your heart open to loss and love simultaneously, knowing you are made for both and they both enhance your life if you invite them in, together.

❋

*My life is made larger through love and loss that tenderly hold
the awareness of each other.*

Recognize the Faces of Grief

The truth of life's impermanence unites us. With perspective we can see that everyone throughout time has had to suffer the reconciliation of love and loss, and to be blessed in ways by the experience. Not to have loved at all would have been the path of greater heartbreak. When we look at people around us, we can see the faces of grief — some wearing it just behind their eyes, some like a cloak. We find ourselves grateful to have such a heart-opening invitation to belong at the center of the shared, unpredictable human story.

Picture yourself held in the embrace of the bereaved, beloved human family. Know that your heart is in communion with the strongest forces of its perseverance in the face of love and loss.

✳

My sorrow and longing connect me to everyone,
everywhere — and them to me.

Acknowledge Love as a Blessing

Loss is not a privilege. But it is helpful to see heartbreak in direct proportion to the love we have offered and received. To have loved at all, to have been loved at all, is a blessing. In the task of finding gifts buried in our loss, we must imagine the emptiness of the alternative, and appreciate the vulnerability that allows us to impact — and to have been impacted by — another. Winnie-the-Pooh knew this when he said, "How lucky I am to have something that makes saying goodbye so hard."

Open your heart to the things that now enrich your life but came from loving something or someone you had to let go. Be grateful to your heart for its beautiful courage.

✳

I carry grief as an evident blessing of having loved and been loved.

Let Your Beliefs Guide Your Grief

Be brave enough to consider your own death. What would you tell the people who gather around you in your final days? What would you tell them about the world that you believe will greet you, and that remains after you are gone? What do you believe about how you will continue to be present to those you love? How would you share these thoughts with them? The ways that you might reassure others offer clear pointers for your principles about loss, but it is challenging to live by their guidance when you are grieving the loss of someone close to you.

Connect with the reassuring ways that you know to make meaning out of the prospect of your own death. Attend to the articulation of beliefs that can offer you and others the gift of reassurance.

✳

Remembering my beliefs about impermanence opens me to more peaceful ways of being with loss.

Pain Opens the Gifts of Pleasure

With our hearts open to pain, we are paradoxically more available to the gifts of pleasure. We may feel raw, but this rawness allows our senses to become more finely attuned. If we can experience the ways that delight travels the same pathways as despair, we see the trove of enriched awareness that waits in our vulnerability. Our senses are opened to the fullness of life when we hear the birds, notice the colors of the sky, taste the sweetness of summer fruit, feel the soft welcome of a pillow, and we are made more whole in our noticing.

Open your senses to those moments that bring joy alongside grief. Allow your availability to beauty to be a balm to your broken heart.

✳

Sorrow opens me to wonder, and I can be faithful to both at the same time.

CHAPTER 10

BELONGING IN NATURE

Into the Woods

November 12, 1993, was marked with a gold star on my wall calendar. It was the date I finished eight months of chemo and radiation and, according to the medical system, was able to consider myself done — for now. I was informed that my risk for recurrence was high, as was the likelihood of a secondary cancer from the treatments, so I was sent on my way on a very short leash: neck-to-pelvis CT scans with dye every three months for two years, then every six months until I hit the five-year mark, then on to annual scans.

The time period immediately after treatment was far more trying than I anticipated. Even if it was fairy-tale thinking, I wanted some semblance of my old energy and well-being back. I struggled to adapt to the limitations of my new body and "chemo brain." Just when I thought I could move beyond such a medicalized life, hope was becoming an occasional and hard-won visitor. The psychic gap between who I felt I was on the inside and what I could actually muster often seemed insurmountable.

After my first three-month scan, I learned that the chief of oncology wanted to meet with me. Even though my results were good, he was concerned about the likelihood of recurrence and suggested I have my bone marrow harvested for a transplant to shore up my odds for survival. I was heartsick. I wanted to live my life, not go through any more procedures to try to ensure it.

"When will I be out of the woods?" I asked, hoping for an exact date to put on my calendar — a date that would hold such promise that I could finally exhale fully. He answered matter-of-factly, "You will never be out of the woods."

Never out of the woods. The words rippled through my mind. With all my focus on surviving the treatment, I had not grasped the degree of uncertainty and struggle that would come afterward. Understanding that my life would only ever come with the caveat of "for now" was sobering. I wondered: How does one continue to live this way? What if there was no way I could plan for the future? What was I able to count on?

I wanted desperately to run away, to live somewhere beyond the grasp of hospitals until I was old and gray. Without even knowing what it meant, I still wanted and felt I deserved some approximation of "normal." I knew I wanted to spend time with people and in places where vulnerability and uncertainty felt normal. Where life and death coexisted and everything was interconnected. Where the ruins and glories of my inner life and body would match the outer world I occupied. If I was never going to be out of the woods, I figured I might as well live in them. I decided then and there to move to the Berkshire hills.

As a girl, I had found solace in the endless acres of wooded land across the street from my house. I would disappear for hours to walk among the maze of tall pines collecting mosses, wintergreen, and ferns for terrariums. Not knowing what was next in my life, I craved that solace and a sense of felt belonging again.

For close to two years, the parameters of my life had been defined by the four walls of the various rooms where I lay in bed. Now, the land would become my home. Moving to a shared, rambling house in a town with 650 residents spread across 21 square miles offered me a needed contrast to the life I had left in New York City. Opening myself to pleasure became my medicine. If I sat still, there was endless living beauty to notice. I found awe and wonder daily with visitations of curious animals, dancing light, and symphonies of birdsong. My senses woke up and came to attention, as if I had been in an extended hibernation. And my body — so accustomed to pain and the anticipation of pain that I had unknowingly shut down its ability to attune to a diverse landscape of sensations and environs — slowly came back to life.

TENDING THE LANDSCAPE OF RECIPROCITY

May you grow still enough to hear the small noises earth makes in preparing for the long sleep of winter, so that you yourself may grow calm and grounded deep within. — Brother David Steindl-Rast

The natural world is the very fabric of life. It is one of the most resplendent and consistent sources of generosity that we will ever know. When we allow ourselves to tune in and pay attention, our Earth is perpetually nourishing and providing for us, sustaining life and offering its abundance with a breathtaking and consistent flourish. We are fed, literally and figuratively, by its offerings every day. Amid fields, rain, trees, flowers, plants, animals, sky, birds, oceans, and sun, we immediately grasp our own relative stature. Feeling inextricably connected yet small in relationship with the natural world can lead us swiftly to a sense of the sacred.

Yet we are living in times when the natural world can seem more and more removed from us, inaccessible to many, and imperiled by humanity's legacy of choices. The offerings of the Earth are woven into our clothing and what we eat, but they are obscured by synthetic ingredients, packaging, factories, and methods of transportation that carry them. These days our gaze is more often directed at a computer, television, or cell phone than at the ground or the sky. As we surrender to each technological advance, it is harder not to be cut off from the thread of connection that helps us know our true and necessary place in the resilient, fragile, reciprocal, real world-wide-web of life. It can require more effort than ever to connect with all that nature holds, and in so many ways it has never been more important — no matter where you live or the "nature" of your life.

Gratefulness supports intentional remembering and honoring of our relationship with Mother Nature. Grateful, we understand the privilege of her offerings and listen for both the small and loud cries for our reverence and stewardship. We allow ourselves to experience the great fullness of our emotions at how inseparable we are from her perpetual flow of gifts, recognize how much and how often we take them for granted, and grieve the losses she is suffering daily at the hands of our "advancing" civilization. Gratefulness invites us to heal our disconnection, live in celebration, and strengthen our place in the rightful relationship of reciprocity with the natural world.

Grateful living asks us to actively engage in ways that respect and also preserve what we treasure most. We are inspired to sustain that which sustains us through remembering the ways that we are bound to the world around us. When we come into union with the generosity of nature, we learn to be humbler and more gracious. As the Persian poet Hafiz says: "After all these years of shining, the sun does not say to the earth, 'you owe me.' . . . Imagine how a love like that can light up the whole world."

BECOME PRESENT TO THE NATURAL WORLD

It is a wholesome and necessary thing for us to turn again to the earth
and in the contemplation of her beauties to know of wonder and humility.
— Rachel Carson

When we lay down the clamoring thoughts of *things* in our lives — things to do and things undone — and when we dare to quiet ourselves in service of communion with the natural world, the peace of our inner landscape matches the quietest outer landscape we can imagine. Stopping to notice the true gifts of our lives — those most freely, consistently, and generously given — we discover again and again the Earth as our great benefactor and most beloved partner. Whenever we take a conscious breath, we know that we are an essential part of the full ecosystem of inspiration.

Deepening a sense of belonging can arouse not only a more reverential engagement with the natural world but can also inform and fortify the ways we relate to ourselves as essential creatures of nature. We are part of a highly interdependent ecology, and when our bonds of connection are strongest we know that to do harm in any one place is to extend harm to many places. To offer the nourishment of our appreciation in any one place is to set a benevolent chain reaction into motion.

We are kin to our precious planet. When we sit, we can embody the tenacious essence of a mountain. Standing, we can embody the balance of a tree. When we lie down, we can become grounded with the blessed Earth. Our heart is pumping blood to keep our bodies alive just as nutrients are pumped through the cells of plants. When we breathe, our breath is a tide touching and releasing the shoreline.

Let us sit, stand, walk, and bow with grateful reverence for the stunning flow of life-giving force that emanates from the Earth's beneficence. Let us offer ourselves with respect and reciprocal care for her perpetual gifts.

❋

What habits, choices, or things take you out of an actively grateful connection with the natural world?

❋

What are some rituals or practices you could add to your life to bring you into a more resonant relationship with nature?

VOICES OF GRATEFUL LIVING

Attentive observation turns me toward a gratitude for my belonging to this earth. Rather than watching from afar, I am allowed to behold the truth of my existence that is right before me. Nature offers me the spacious blessing to be a witness to the world and know that I am connected to all of it. Gratitude arises as nature pronounces that I am not only included, but necessary. Gratitude nurtures the ever-present rhythm of nature. A rhythm that inherently includes my heart, my breath, my mind, and all that is.
— Tom M.

SEEK A PERSPECTIVE OF WONDER AND REVERENCE

My religion is nature. That's what arouses those feelings of wonder and mysticism and gratitude in me. — Oliver Sacks

All manner of things born of the Earth can awaken us to perspective. And our moments in nature can offer us gratitude for life's preciousness and remind us of our fragile, powerful bonds of connection.

Look up. Taking the time to truly notice a sunset, starry sky, sunrise, or the clouds above our heads can grant immediate perspective on our lives and reconnect us with astonishment. Look closely. A stone, flower, feather, ladybug, leaf, or snowflake can capture our senses and deliver a sense of wonder.

Look out. Gazing into the canopy of a tree, into the eyes of a beloved animal, across a farm field, or at sunlight coming through a window can bring reverence. The daisy pushing itself through the smallest crack in the pavement, the squirrel leaping from one branch to another, the rainbow at the intersection point of rain and sun — let us be in awe of nature's tenacious resilience, and the ways that life so often leans toward the light. The Earth is a gifted, generous teacher, and we are wise to be her students, as she has been around far longer and been through far more than we have been.

To turn our gaze inward with that same appreciative perspective would be a most spectacular thing. No less *natural* than the hills and valleys, fields and forests, flowers and clouds, we can be dazzled by ourselves and each other. We can observe the comings and goings of our feeling-states and thoughts, growth and loss, relationships, darkness and light, with the same appreciation and curiosity as we do the seasons and clouds. With our senses awake, our interest piqued for all that already is and all that will unfold, we can know ourselves as fully present to, and a full participant in, our mysterious experience of life.

Having these kinds of peak experiences, says Brother David, connects us to a kind of everyday mysticism and unites us in a sense of oneness and limitless belonging that helps us maintain perspective. To enjoy a peak experience and the viewpoint it offers, it helps to summit an actual mountaintop, but it is rare that we can scale such literal peaks. Instead, we can gain a richer perspective through the infinite landscape of our attention and the environment of our imaginations, in any moment of our lives.

✷

What direct experiences, memories, and imaginings in nature
bring you into a sense of wonder or awe?

✷

What instills a sense of reverence in you? When and where are you
most likely to experience reverence in the natural world?

AWAKEN POSSIBILITY FOR THE NATURAL WORLD

When we drop fear, we can draw nearer to people, we can draw nearer to the Earth, we can draw nearer to all the heavenly creatures that surround us. — bell hooks

To discover possibility for our natural world requires that we feel our connection and interdependence with our whole hearts. As is so often the case, gratefulness will ask us to tune in, lean in, and listen. We will need to embrace uncomfortable feelings in ourselves, as we may hear a lament from the roots of the trees, a cry from our Mother's creatures, a roar from her oceans. Love for our Earth will crack our hearts open, as it should, and leave us seeking new ways of being in concert with life.

Nature is not a one-way relationship built for our pure enjoyment, entertainment, and comfort. A new possibility will require us to go beyond a relationship of usefulness and service. If we do not commit to a deep-seated, reciprocal regard, we will extract pleasure and utility to the point of no return.

The Earth needs us to act — rooted in our passion — for her preservation and protection. We are her keepers and caretakers. To live in true honor of the natural world will require us to be inconvenienced and less efficient at times. Beyond taking simple actions like swapping out our lightbulbs, we may have to completely reinvent aspects of our lives that cost our world too much and put us out of alignment with our values. Transportation, travel, leisure, lifestyles, consumption, and how we get our food, from where, and when — much of it may need reconsideration and change. The more we let ourselves feel love and gratitude for our natural world, the more grief and responsibility we are likely to feel. It is worth every iota of our heartbroken consideration to be part of a new possibility for the Earth.

Envisioning new ways of being in stewardship with the Earth will invite us to explore far-reaching conversations about sustainability. We need to do this in concert with others, in community, in circles, on farmland, at the edges of oceans, in urban parks and at the base of skyscrapers as well as under majestic trees. Everything is up for consideration, including what we need versus what we want, and what is essential versus the lifestyle to which we have become accustomed. At the center of the circle are the questions "What is my share of the pie?" and "With whom can I share the pie?" and "How can I be more grateful for having a pie at all?"

✳

What are some ways that you currently demonstrate and share your love for our planet? What are some ways you give back? Is this a different form of loving?

✳

What could you do to up-level the ways that you show grateful care for the Earth?

What I Want and What I Can Have

After dinner, I try to digest
kale and cauliflower in my longing
to live longer, and a root-beer float
in case my world ends tomorrow.
I play the gamble game with exercise
and diet, reminded daily by obituaries
featuring people younger than me:
the impossible becoming likely.
I want to go out full, embraced by my life,
the grand quilt of being here. Yet memories
are remnants, and come one patch at a time.
And like moments, most fade unnoticed.
After a storm, I take a walk.
At the jasmine vine by my front door,
a raindrop, suspended on a stem, stops me.
What I want, what I can have, merge.
— Jeanie Greensfelder

VOICES OF GRATEFUL LIVING

I am so profoundly thankful for the natural world and wilderness I am so lucky to live beside and within. I live in Southern Chile, and this land and place is a blessing in so many ways. The forests are so incredibly generous, with their cool shade on hot days, and the abundance of food they offer through every season — so many medicinal plants, roots, leaves, also plenty of edible mushrooms, berries, and fruits grow wildly in abundance. The sheer beauty of the wildness that remains here steals my breath literally every morning. Each day there is a quiet celebration for this Earth.
— Greta M.

GRATEFUL FOR EACH MOMENT

For the Earth to stay in balance, for the gifts to continue to flow, we must give back in equal measure for what we are given. Our first responsibility, the most potent offering we possess, is gratitude. — Robin Wall Kimmerer

Nature is one of our most consistent sources of inspiration for gratefulness. When we encounter her majesty, we encounter the sacred paradox of our own significance and smallness. The natural world casts us into reverence. We are both lost and found there, and we are nourished in every moment of every day.

Grateful living inspires us to sustain that which sustains us. It is vital to be in a reciprocal, life-giving relationship with our Mother Earth and to experience our inextricability with her at all times. Our pain and joy are connected and true, and both are needed for the healing and repair of our world.

✳

May you hold the gifts of nature with wonder and reverence.

Practices and Prompts

STOP. LOOK. GO. PRACTICE
Be the Earth

Just as we need to listen in order to be in healthy relationship with each other, we need to attune ourselves toward the Earth as well. We need to open ourselves to be impacted, informed, and inspired. Sometimes it can be helpful to make a sincere effort to listen to the Earth and hear what she has to tell us.

> **Stop:** Sit comfortably with a journal and do the All Breathe practice (page 169). Attune your body and the natural world to breathe and beat synchronously.

> **Look:** Imagine yourself as intimately belonging to the Earth. In any way that you can, take a peak awareness perspective of our planet or some aspect of the Earth that allows you to experience empathic attunement. Take a few minutes to find yourself in a felt oneness.

> Now, endeavor to let the Earth speak to you. Open your heart and put yourself into a receptive conversation with our planetary home. Suspend any judgment or awkwardness that may put distance between you and this experience. Let yourself listen intently to the Earth as you imagine that she speaks and asks of you:

> *I need your love. How do you love me?*

> *I need your gratitude. What do you appreciate most about me?*

> *I need your care. How do you want to care for me?*

> *I need your protection. How will you protect me?*

> *I need your courage. How will you be bold for me?*

> *I need your creativity. How will you create a new future for me?*

> **Go:** Write down your responses, and then make a plan for how your answers could become actionable. Share your list with someone, or do this practice with a group of people and share your responses. Begin doing something every day that lets the Earth know that she has been heard and is cherished.

All Breathe

Close your eyes and take a few slow, full breaths. Be aware that count-less plants and trees all over the Earth have contributed to creating the oxygen that is nourishing your body through your lungs. Breathing in, remember that on every continent, in every town, everything alive is breathing with you. Breathing out, remember that plants help us breathe by taking in carbon dioxide and letting oxygen out. We are part of a benevolent cycle. When you see plants and trees, remember they are your lifeline to aliveness. Let this reality keep you apprecia-tively amazed and inspired.

A Special Space

Imagine yourself somewhere that awakens your sense of communion with the glories of our Earth. What spot on our planet gives rise to a feeling of peace and well-being for you? Give this place a name. What do you most appreciate? What do you notice when you are there? Look up. Look down. Describe both the distant landscape and the details you see if you look closely. What is your felt sense of this place? What feelings arise when you imagine being here?

When you have a strong sense of a place in nature you would call "home," think about the kinds of things that threaten this spot. What kinds of forces is this place susceptible to? Are there things that imperil the sustainability of this place? When our practice carries us from *Stop* and *Look* to Go, our gratitude moves us to do something. When you imagine the sacred places in nature you are grateful for, as well as their vulnerability, what do you feel inspired to do to protect them? Think of some small acts to protect the natural world you cher-ish. Now think of how you could go and act on them.

PERSPECTIVE PROMPTS
Awaken to Connectedness

When we see the Earth as an exquisitely fragile ecosystem on which all of humanity relies, we feel our interconnectedness. When something hap-pens to any one piece of the system, it impacts the whole. In every moment, everything in nature serves our human aliveness in countless ways, just as we are able to serve or hurt the natural world with our choices. No one of us is any less a part of nature than any other. When Mother Earth cries out for care, she is calling on us. When we need care, we may be needing her. All of life is interwoven.

As you awaken to the susceptibility and generosity of the natural world, feel the fragile threads that weave us all together, and know your presence makes a difference.

*

My well-being is connected to the well-being of the Earth in every minute of every day.

Hold a Vast View

When astronauts look from space, they see the beauty of our planet with new eyes. If we have traveled by plane, we have glimpsed a view of the Earth that inspires amazement and belonging. If we hold a vast view of our planet, it can strike us as even more miraculous that it is the only one in our solar system that we know for sure is able to support life. It can overwhelm us with wonder to understand all the forces in nature that have to come together to keep our Earth functioning, and to support her billions of diverse inhabitants. Surprise and wonder await us whenever we behold the miracle of life on Earth.

Envision yourself gazing at our planet from a distance above. Behold the faces of people turned up toward you and the sky with reverence for the miracle.

*

Life on this Earth is miraculous, and I hold it in my heart and hands.

Acknowledge Earth's Generosity

The natural world is constantly providing us nourishment in both seen and unseen ways. There is such a glorious abundance surrounding us in every moment. No matter where we live, the Earth helps to keep us breathing so we will not expire. We are inspired every time we open our hearts and senses! We are provided food from the Earth's riches. Trees, plants, herbs, roots, water — all blessings. Even under threat, the Earth remains generous. Awakening to the extraordinary wonders and plenty of the natural world, we can be ever grateful.

When you are next enjoying a meal, consider how many different ingredients arose from the Earth. Think of how your nourishment is provided for. Say a blessing of thanksgiving.

✻

The natural world generously provides for me in extraordinary ways every day.

Follow Your Values

Most of us have daily behaviors that express our values about the environment. We might recycle cans and bottles, bring reusable bags to the grocery store, or use biodegradable products. Maybe you belong to a food co-op or buy from your local farmer's market. Additionally, it is important to listen for what else might be needed in order to be in alignment with our values. What do our most deeply held beliefs ask us to consider about how we behave and belong in the natural world? What truly matters to us? How do we offer our attention and appreciation to what matters most?

Know that every little thing you do and choice you make can take you into or out of alignment with your value of the Earth's well-being. Commit to doing a little more to better love what you value, and value what you love.

✻

My value of the Earth compels me to tend those things for which I am most grateful.

Tune In to Magnificence

We too often take natural beauty for granted. Stuck in feeling deprived or disappointed by life, we walk by her splendor without noticing. Meanwhile, nature is busy every moment creating magnificence that brings us hope and delights our senses. A sunrise and birdsong start our day, a tree growing through pavement moves us to hope, perennials commit to us even if we move away, and plants say "breathe" and make it all possible. Our senses attune us to creation, creativity, and celebration. How much more pleasure could we want? How much more alive could we feel?

Stop to look for nature's tenacity and magnificence more often. Look up. Look down. Look out. When you discover it, make time to study it more closely. Be still and let yourself be moved.

※

Everywhere I look, the Earth is offering its magnificent beauty and hope.

CHAPTER 11

CELEBRATING SUFFICIENCY

Appreciated Assets

By the time I finished all my cancer treatments, I had no money. Nothing in my savings or checking accounts. No stash under the mattress. No equity. No home or car. Certainly no investments or retirement fund. And no job. I was living on $731 a month from Social Security Disability Income and still had thousands of dollars in outstanding hospital bills to pay. By any traditional standards, I was broke. But with less money than at any other time in my adult life, I felt incredibly rich.

After spending time anticipating not being alive, the riches of life were abundant. I noticed the preciousness of each and every thing. A roof over my head. Clothes, and a body to wear them. Medical advances, care providers, alternative treatments. Skin. Touch. Friends, family, mentors. The breathtaking beauty of the natural world, the taste of food, a warm bed. Taking nothing for granted, I could not believe that I still had the gift of being alive and the even greater privilege of knowing that life was the one true gift that allowed for all others.

My experience seemed to put me way out of step with others around me. Many of my peers were focused on things I no longer had an interest in: accumulating money and fancy things, professional ambitions, buying a home, starting a family, and the expectation of longevity to be able to contain it all. The focus on external markers of happiness and success that seemed so important in the culture at large were lost on me, and I found myself disoriented — out of the running, so to speak.

I had gotten a glimpse of what mattered and what we could take with us in the end, and little of it was reflected in how I used to live and how so many others were living. The lure of a distant future that would bring fulfillment was something I simply could not bank on, financially or otherwise. As I entered my posttreatment life, a nurse told me that my new peer group was people in their seventies and eighties — my grandparents' age. I could sense the truth of this. I felt more kinship with folks whose definition of long-term planning was calculated in months, not years or decades, people who celebrated the simple pleasures of their days at hand without counting on more.

The wealth from which I benefited most was relational. "Community" is what I came to call my real *social* security. A generosity I hardly knew possible began holding and carrying me. Baskets of vegetables and berries came from acquaintances whose gardens overflowed, an exercise bicycle came from a neighbor, warm meals arrived at the door, rides were offered, the driveway was plowed for free. I benefited every day from a stealth "care economy," an underworld of unconditional kindness as currency. No debt or indebtedness allowed. I was suddenly at the center of a community of sharing and cooperation that was shoring me up and helping me get through life. Not only that, it fed me in ways that enlivened a sense of possibility for everyone involved, and for a generous, interdependent future we could all imagine.

Surviving cancer taught me to notice all that is available here and now, to see beyond the myth that more is better, and to make a practice of not taking life and love for granted. The harbinger of joy is to focus on noticing, appreciating, sharing more of what is already given and present. Absent that capacity for appreciating what *is*, more of anything ultimately ends up neglected or as landfill. It was clear to me: life is meant to be savored, for as long as we are able, as often as we are able, in relationship to as many experiences as we are able.

THE WEALTH OF WHAT ALREADY IS

We have thousands of opportunities every day to be grateful. There's opportunity upon opportunity to be grateful; that's what life is.
— Brother David Steindl-Rast

Grateful living is a powerful antidote to our feelings of scarcity. As Lynne Twist, founder of the Soul of Money Institute, says: "What we appreciate appreciates." When we value the gifts we already have and offer them our attention, they flourish and offer us more in return. When we trade our acquisitive tendencies for appreciative tendencies, the experience of *enoughness* — which brings ease and equanimity to our lives and relationships — can offer more than having "more" will ever deliver. Cultivating the conditions of inner contentment can simplify our needs and help us find that "just enough" is actually plenty.

While our longings for more may be rooted in a deep-seated yearning for greater meaning at the center of our lives, the way these longings show up is often as a pervasive sense of lack and dissatisfaction with what we have, what we are, and what is.

There is a felt sufficiency to life that can offer us far greater rewards than any material goods or money can bring. Ironically, the more money and things we end up managing, the more difficult it can be to remember and access the true abundance of things that matter most to us.

While we should never deny true unmet needs or the valid challenges that can arise from not having what we need, we can still significantly increase our well-being through an intentional focus on noticing what we do have. Being present to our lives as they are is essential. If we cannot savor the things that right in front of us, right at our fingertips, how could having *more* possibly make us happy? Or, how could we possibly understand and move toward the *more* that we actually need if we are not present to what we already have? Settling into the wealth of our lives as they are opens us to better appreciate what is, and whatever will be.

BECOME PRESENT TO SUFFICIENCY

Acknowledging the good that is already in your life is the foundation for all abundance. — Eckhart Tolle

Being alive in this particular moment affords us many gifts of civilization, such as electricity, running water, central heat, air conditioning, and other advancements our grandparents would have thought pure science fiction. Our money is available 24 hours a day anywhere in the world, a phone the size of a deck of cards can connect us to those we love anytime, and immediate answers to any question we might ponder is just one click away. Not to mention electric cars, air travel, solar panels, and medical advances. How could our ancestors have imagined the extent of our conveniences and luxuries? All of it is truly extraordinary, and most of us want to more fully treasure it. In our hearts, we yearn to notice, treasure, and invest in what is already in our life. But despite our best intentions, it is difficult to fulfill this aspiration.

The societal messages that barrage us in our commercialized world encourage us to perseverate about what could be and fixate on the future, negating the sacred fullness of our present moments. We are encouraged to move fast and want more; to cling, grasp, crave, and covet; to take what we have for granted in the pursuit of more, different, and better. All of this leads to getting caught on the hamster wheel of life, forgetting again and again that the present moment is truly all we have, and it is precious and fleeting.

At our core, we know life is precious and short, and so our hearts long for us to be here now, and happy. This will require us to be in touch with the poignancy of the ever-passing present moment and to live it fully and gratefully. We bless ourselves with contentment when we recognize the blessings of the things and moments available to us now. Appreciating the abundant gifts of life that we already have is a reliable pathway to satisfaction and joy.

✳

How do you know when you have enough of something?
What does sufficiency feel like?

✳

What are ten things that are truly sufficient in your life right now?

VOICES OF GRATEFUL LIVING
The moment I stop and look from the position of gratitude, I've lined myself up with Flow and the world transforms before me. Each day of this practice builds on the previous in such a way that there is rarely a day that I am not struck by the innumerable blessings all around. Somehow, I've always intuitively known that each moment of simple existence is something to be utterly grateful for, the foundation for all real experience and knowing, and the place from which to be drenched in joy every day.
— Craig I.

SEEK A PERSPECTIVE OF CONTENTMENT AND CELEBRATION

Gratitude unlocks the fullness of life. It turns what we have into enough, and more. — Melody Beattie

Why do we so often feel that life is not delivering enough of what we want, need, or expect? Why do we feel that we do not have enough or that we may not *be* enough? Why do we routinely walk past our blessings without acknowledging them? How is it possible to feel so much scarcity when we are surrounded and filled by so much plenty?

Paradoxically, the more developed and affluent a society, the more we will be on the receiving end of messages telling us we do not have enough. It can be helpful to remember that this discontent is intentionally manufactured and targeted at us. The messages of lack can keep us invested in illusions of inadequacy and stuck in insatiability, no matter what we have. We aspire and acquire and end up empty.

Cultural messages that instill a sense of scarcity are insidious. They are so constant that they are scarcely discernible as propaganda — they are more like the air that we breathe. Inhale: Something about my life is not enough. Exhale: If only I had X or was more Y, life would be so much better. In response, many of us become impostors, spending money we do not have or pretending we have less than we really have to hide our actual ease. Either way, our moments of felt sufficiency are dwarfed by felt scarcity, and then we suffer the additional discomfort of not feeling truly seen or known. The experience of residing within a scarcity economy cuts across class lines and is prevalent in nearly all developed societies.

We have a tendency, in order to bond with each other, to turn away from acknowledging the ways in which we are gratified or grateful, and instead allow scarcity to lead the conversation. Often, if we are longing for an immediate sense of belonging, we can initiate a conversation focused on the things that feel insufficient or lacking in our lives. And commiseration awaits us! Think of the common ground of "not good enough" that we can talk about: work, pay, retirement funds, health, relationships, sleep, intimacy, body image, weather . . . on and on. And, of course, the greatest "never enough": Time. Time off, time for work, time to play, time to rest, time for love, time to live. All the while, we miss being present to the time that we do have.

The quest for more can blind us to what is already, actually plenty. We see this in children who, anticipating the next wrapped gift, have already forgotten the one they just opened. This plays out for adults, too. Each time we find ourselves thinking about dessert or our next meal while still eating dinner, or miss truly hearing what someone is saying because we are planning our response, we become unable to celebrate whatever is coming our way because we focus on what could be. We have fallen prey to missing the beauty of what is present for the lure of the imagined possible. FOMO (fear of missing out) is more and more common. It is easy to get caught in the myths of all that we might be missing because we are incessantly told that the grass is always greener just beyond where we are.

✳

What are things you can count on to bring you true contentment?

✳

When and with whom do you feel liberated from a sense of scarcity?

AWAKEN THE POSSIBILITY OF SUFFICIENCY

In ordinary life we hardly realize that we receive a great deal more than
we give, and that it is only with gratitude that life becomes rich.
— Dietrich Bonhoeffer

Living in a society that weaves its livelihood from the threads of our felt scarcity and discontent makes daring to explore sufficiency and contentment a rather radical proposition. But possibilities for exploring this commitment are everywhere. One of the first places we can start is by celebrating and appreciating all that is good and full about our lives, and to begin to risk doing so aloud and through our actions. We can change our lives through changing the thoughts and conversations we have about our lives — and in doing so, we inspire others to do the same.

Grateful living invites us to savor and share what we have — living more simply so that others might simply live. Appreciation for what we have is a powerful first step to contentment and offers the possibility of sustainability for others and life on our planet. Think about how much you have that you cannot or do not actively appreciate. Things that sit on shelves behind other things. Items that are gathering dust. Stuff you may be holding on to for sentimental reasons but never look at. Things in storage spaces. Knowing that everything you own will need to be dealt with when you are no longer alive (or even if you move), what do you have that is more than you truly want and need? If we have more material goods than we can actively appreciate, we can recognize that sharing our underappreciated treasures can allow these items to get the use and appreciation that they need and deserve. Redistributing our "fortune" for the benefit of the whole enriches us, others, and our neglected blessings sitting in wait.

❋

What do you have that is longing to be more appreciated? Do you
know others who could offer that appreciation better than you can?

❋

Once you begin to more fully appreciate what you have, what might
your contentment reveal to you?

VOICES OF GRATEFUL LIVING
Gratefulness keeps my mind balanced, so my heart and hands give more
easily. — Beatrice K.

MY SYMPHONY
To live content with small means.
To seek elegance rather than luxury,
and refinement rather than fashion.
To be worthy not respectable,
and wealthy not rich.
To study hard, think quietly, talk gently,
act frankly, to listen to stars, birds, babes,
and sages with open heart, to bear all cheerfully,
do all bravely, await occasions, hurry never.
In a word, to let the spiritual,
unbidden and unconscious,
grow up through the common.
This is to be my symphony.
— William Ellery Channing

GRATEFUL FOR EACH MOMENT

When you let go of trying to get more of what you don't really need, it frees
up oceans of energy to make a difference with what you have. — Lynne Twist

The habits of mind and behavior that keep us on the treadmill of "more is
better" can be intractable, especially living in a culture that defines us by what
we do and have rather than who we are. A sense of scarcity and urgency is
so commonplace that we can hardly imagine being energized or motivated
without it — but it keeps us less resilient and resourceful. Many of us long
for unconditional well-being but lack guidance about ways to cultivate and
experience it.

Grateful living is a direct pathway to the qualities of mind and heart that lend themselves to well-being and sustainability. Simple living emerges organically when we trade our acquisitive tendencies for appreciative ones. Then the experience of enoughness, which brings peace and equanimity to our lives and relationships, spills over into an experience of true abundance.

✹

May you hold your life with contentment and celebration.

Practices and Prompts

STOP. LOOK. GO. PRACTICE
Put on Your Perspectacles

Author, activist, and philanthropist Glennon Doyle describes shifting the lens through which she looks at her life to gain perspective and appreciation as putting on her "perspectacles." She writes, "Today I shall keep my perspectacles super-glued to my face and feel insanely grateful instead of lacking. I will look at my home and my people and my body and say: Thank you. Thank you, thank you, thank you. This is all more than good enough, all of it. Now. Let us turn our focus onward and outward. There is work to be done and joy to be had." We can follow her example.

Stop: Stop whatever you are doing and devote your full attention to being still or slowing down. Notice how you are nourished and renewed by the flow of air in your lungs. Bring your awareness to the present moment and allow yourself to soften into it.

Look: Look around the place where you live. Notice that you have a place to live. Try to see it through new, unaccustomed eyes. Imagine someone coming to visit who has a great deal less than you do. Imagine yourself showing that person where you live, taking them through each space, feeling true gratitude for what is yours to share. Now focus on the kitchen. Imagine that it is completely empty or that it does not exist at all. See empty cupboards, counters, and drawers in your mind's eye. What would change if you did not have what you have? What does this place offer you and others in your life?

Go: Write a list of what you value in your kitchen. Appreciate the faucet, stove, and spoons. Refrigerator, coffeemaker, tea kettle. Note what you love and use most. Remind yourself to appreciate things you use every day.

- Draw a heart on beloved items with an erasable pen, or a permanent one if you feel brave. Or put a heart sticker on it or a Post-it note with the word *gift*. If you live with others, explain that you are on an appreciation campaign, and invite them to join in.

- For one week, keep a bag or box in your kitchen or hallway. Whenever you notice something that is not used, more than you need, or something not fully appreciated, put the item in the box. Invite others in your household to offer things as well. This can spark meaningful conversations about living simply. Redistribute your good fortune.

- Offer to share items you don't use often with neighbors and friends: tools, infrequently used kitchen items like food dehydrators, even your vegetable garden. Not everyone needs one of everything — especially these kinds of things.

- How would taking nothing for granted in your kitchen change how you move through the space? How would you use and enjoy it differently? What can you do to creatively remind yourself about the ways in which you are fortunate?

Envy Turnaround

Envy is an important source of information about our longings, but it separates us from our contentment and can wreak havoc on our connections with others. Feeling inspired connects us with people whose lives embody what we desire. Whenever you experience tinges of envy, turn it into inspiration. Practice noticing and saying to yourself, "I am so inspired by . . ." Become aware of how this shift impacts your sense of opportunity and possibility. As an added practice, tell a person who has helped you connect with one of your true longings how inspired you are by their example.

Shifting the Conversation to Sufficiency

When you find yourself in conversations that keep gravitating toward complaining or perseverating in unconstructive ways, try to make gentle shifts in the conversation. Honoring our human need for commiseration and compassion, there are ways to redirect people toward noticing the resources we all have. Conversational interventions that help to remind people of what they have going for them can be supportive in dealing with what we feel so readily is not going our way. The point of this practice is to change *your* language, not to change someone else's. Model what it can look like to be vulnerable and grateful at the same time. Intervene in your own propensities to focus on what might be lacking. Inspire others to notice the gifts in their lives by remarking on those you appreciate in yours.

PERSPECTIVE PROMPTS
Embrace the Ephemeral

Everything we can touch is impermanent. Nothing we purchase will last. No matter how identified we are with the things we own, all objects are actually ephemeral and could go away at any moment. Wake-up call experiences remind us of this, and we are lucky if we receive warnings and teachings as opposed to more significant losses. Fires, floods, storms, accidents — these are occasions when we are reminded of what really matters and endures.

Consider how you could look at all the stuff you own that would not survive a flood or fire, versus what will last beyond you. What matters most to you? Be sure to "own" that.

✳

I am investing in the gifts in life that matter to me, and last.

See the Mundane Anew

Being able to more fully appreciate what we have is vital to living a grateful life. Brother David says that "the greatest surprise is that there is anything at all." Consider this possibility: anything that does not surprise you may be something you are taking for granted. You can walk through your days dulled by expectations and degrees of entitlement, or you can look with a more objective perspective and realize that everything you have become accustomed to is indeed a gift and a blessing.

Imagine yourself being "gifted" each thing you currently own, each item wrapped and delivered with care. Newly experienced, how you might celebrate what you already have?

❊

I am blessed beyond imagining when I treat what I already have
as a surprise.

Take a Big-Picture View

We can gain perspective on our relative riches by reminding ourselves that this moment in time affords us the greatest access to resources, technology, comforts, and conveniences of any time in history. As members of a global family and residents of our one true home, planet Earth, remember to take a big-picture view and consider that if you have food in a refrigerator, clothes in a closet, a bed to sleep on, and a roof over your head, you are among only about 25 percent of the entire global village.

Allow this relative frame of reference to impact you with a sense of gratitude for all the things you benefit from, especially within the context of our larger global family.

❊

My good fortune is extraordinary when considered in relative terms.

Be a Citizen Rather than a Consumer

Gratefulness is a direct pathway to qualities of mind and heart that commit us to living in ways that cast a lighter footprint, consume fewer nonrenewable resources, allocate money in alignment with our values, and unleash generosity. When we act merely as consumers, we stop behaving like citizens who can have an impact with our time, choices, and resources. When we live by our principles and tend what we value, a sense of felt sufficiency frees us up to consider the needs of others and to participate in shaping the world in which we live.

Consider how you could more deeply align your lifestyle choices with your core values and have a greater experience of sufficiency. Consider what you could do and give from your abundance.

✳

Claiming my contentment is healing for myself and the world.

Make Each Day a Banquet

Enjoying what is available to you is key to grateful living. You can turn away from a sense of lack and turn your attention toward the symphony that life is playing for you. You can revel in music, art, light, darkness, your senses, human and animal companions, silence, poetry, surprise. You can love who and what you love. How are you being invited to enjoy what is yours to enjoy? How can giving yourself permission to more fully celebrate and share what is in your life right now make your days a banquet?

Gratefulness is emboldened in moments of ease and enjoyment. Your unmitigated joys will help you have resilience and wisdom in facing challenges. So treasure your pleasures, and share your wealth!

✳

Enjoying my life whenever I can is a form of generosity — toward myself and others.

CHAPTER 12

HEALING A
HURTING WORLD

On Tender Hooks

The first two years of surviving cancer were measured in minutes, days, and weeks. Minutes were both ecstatic and excruciating, allowing me to notice an emotional continuum I had never before experienced. Days were strings of consecutive moments: each morning's awakening an epiphany — blinking my eyes, running my hands over my face and neck just to convince myself it was truly still me, incarnate. Each night marked a victory and an exhausted prayer for another day. Weeks encompased seven days of revelation. And then I finally began to think in months. They became my measure to calculate hope for survival and a big leap from counting the hours when I was going through treatment. But a year? A year had come to feel like a thousand months.

At first, there was a palpable intensity to my moments as they were focused in such detail on the opportunity of living and the possibility of dying. Everything was foreground. Everything was lived in the *now* — unbearably urgent and unsustainably vivid. But as the weeks turned into months and 12 months became my first year, I started to think of cancer more like a chronic disease — one whose absence, presence, or possibility would keep me company for as long as I lived. I reconciled myself to there not being a cure but, instead, opportunities to heal and live every day.

When I reached the two-year survival mark and got a clear CT scan, I had a party. We celebrated the fact that I had reached a hopeful juncture and was able to wait a full six months between scans. But it was disorienting. What to do with all that time? Even if I counted the prep, recovery, and waiting period for results from each scan as taking about a month of my life, I now had ten whole months out of every year that I would not have to plan to go to the hospital.

I wrote this in a letter to friends and family: *In late summer, I had my two-year check-up at the hospital. It was, I think, the most nervous I have felt. It struck me then, and still does, that to long for life so fully, to want it with all your heart, is the victory that can never be taken away. And it is made all that much more poignant by choosing to live in a way that — no matter when the end — we have the most to lose. To constrict, to turn away, to close our doors so that the losing of life or love will be less painful, so that there will be less longed for and therefore less lost — this is the life that fear beckons us to live — the life that, while feeling safe, is not truly lived at all.*

I had focused so intensely on living one moment at a time and trying to make it to my two-year anniversary that I had, for all intents and purposes, forgotten to plan my life. I marked my calendar with hospital tests and doctor appointments like some people do their meal planning. Then I came to a cliff of sorts and hovered at the edge. I had spent so long trying to stay alive, and now I needed to learn to live in a way that allowed for the possibility of a future — even a near future.

What does one do with an unexpected second chance? I knew that there was no going back. My old life was gone, and even though some of my survivor buddies wanted nothing more than to rejoin the trajectory of their previous life and be their old selves again, I could not fathom such a possibility. Nothing about me fit into my old attire — literally or figuratively. I wanted my life to reflect and offer up my learning in some significant way, but I did not know what that was.

Before getting sick, I had been working in the social change nonprofit sector. I was accustomed to having a professional life that reflected my values, but it had become harder to know what that meant. How had my values changed? What had I learned? Who was I professionally after this long work hiatus and all that I had been through? And how would I apply for a job when I was not sure I would be alive in a year or two? How could I sign an employment contract in good conscience? How would I navigate questions about my long-term goals? How did I ever do any of those things before?

Not having answers, I did the only thing I could imagine: I applied for work at my local hospice. Just as moving to the woods surrounded me with the wide-open questions and answers of the land, I knew that going to work for hospice would put me among people who could accompany me in the conversations and commitments that had become most meaningful. My approach to social change had morphed. While I had previously focused on systemic change, I now saw the ways that individuals, friends, families, and communities formed their own systems that could transform within a healing death experience. It meant the world to me that people who chose to work for hospice could hold space for the fact that I had been awakened to my mortality, and all of what that might mean. Also, I had come to value hospice as a radical intervention in the medical system. Over the years I had been sick, in treatment and then in recovery, I had seen clearly the ripple effects of a death with hospice and one without it.

Surviving cancer made me want to channel my good fortune and gratitude into service. Focusing on supporting people at their end of life was the most worthwhile way that I could imagine turning my experience to benefit others. Grateful for all the love and care I had received when the quantity of my life was in question, I was moved to help offer quality of life to others.

THE ART OF GRATEFUL GUARDIANSHIP

Gratefulness will be that full response which releases the full power of my compassion. Gratefulness is creative and overflows into action. — Brother David Steindl-Rast

Suffering has long existed in our world, and along with it the sources of that suffering, from individualized to institutionalized. Whether we have experienced discrimination, violence, or poverty ourselves, we are all impacted. Some of us sadly more than others. Many of us experience the struggles of the human condition both externally and from within. We want desperately to make a positive difference in the world — yet, facing suffering and so many competing needs, our feelings of heartbreak, outrage, or powerlessness often lead to exhaustion or overwhelm. While trying to do the right thing, we can perseverate about what to do without actually doing much at all. Or we try to do so much that we end up overwrought and depleted. Even if we know that we want major change to happen, we might lack clarity about how to focus our energy and actions to have the positive impact we desire.

When we deeply feel the hurts of the world, it can be hard to know how to make a positive difference. How do we best care for our diverse global family? How do we offer healing and repair to others, especially when we ourselves feel in need? How do we act when our hearts are so broken and the world feels so broken? What do we do when we do not know what to do?

Grateful living offers us significant support and direction. The more we allow our hearts to expand and feel inextricably tied to the places and people of this world, the more we will be moved to take a stand on behalf of what we value. Our work is to befriend ourselves, to know our essential belonging, to keep opening ourselves to include more of the world as our beloved own, and to learn to follow our hearts as they move us toward action.

BECOME PRESENT TO A HURTING WORLD

Do not be dismayed by the brokenness of the world. All things break. And all things can be mended. Not with time, as they say, but with intention. So, go. Love intentionally, extravagantly, unconditionally. The broken world waits in darkness for the light that is you. — L. R. Knost

There are days when being awake to the conditions of our world is more than we feel able to bear. We may be called to face outrage, fear, overwhelm, heartbreak, and powerlessness — a difficult mix of feelings even on a good day. We might feel like we want to wait until our grief and anger dissipate before we act — but we could be waiting forever. While our feelings can be overpowering, they can also motivate important action and change. We need to remember to be grateful for our ability to feel. Brokenheartedness means we are alive. Empathy is a blessing that connects us to others. It is a privilege to be informed and to have a sense of protective outrage. We are fortunate to be able to notice and accept with open eyes and an open heart that there are things that are unacceptable. Not to feel all of this would be a true brokenness. Holding gratitude for our deepest feelings is critical as we approach being present to what breaks our hearts open.

In many ways, becoming present to our hurting world is similar to coming into greater presence with ourselves when we are suffering, and others when they are. We tune in, we lean in, and we listen in. We hold the awareness of a hurting world with the same qualities of attention we bring to appreciating our emotional landscapes and unleashing the gifts of our relationships: compassion, curiosity, humility, generosity of spirit. We make ourselves available and allow ourselves to be impacted.

As Tennessee Williams says, "The world will have its way with you. We are saved only by love — love for each other and the love that we pour into the art we feel compelled to share: being a parent; being a writer; being a painter; being a friend. We live in a perpetually burning building, and what we must save from it, all the time, is love."

One of the gifts of love is that it is a renewable resource, an endless spring of nourishment. Love is a force that motivates action, and we know well how to heed it as a source of inspiration. So let's pledge to be present to love. To feel vulnerable, with love. To grieve, with love. To be heartbroken, with love. To be afraid, with love. To be shattered by love. To be grateful for love. And to keep listening to this source, feeling and trusting what is called forth and called for — what we, with our broken hearts, can do from love to help heal our hurting world.

＊

What can you allow love to do through you today to make a difference
in the areas where you see or feel hurting?

＊

How could you make it an art to approach everything you see and do
from your heart, your art? How might this change how you approach
what you do?

> **VOICES OF GRATEFUL LIVING**
> Being mindful of approaching life with gratitude and being grateful for the
> circumstances of my life creates its own subtle, yet sustained energy. That
> energy, combined with knowledge and will, joins forces that can, if applied,
> affect the need for social change around me. — Kevin L.

SEEK A PERSPECTIVE OF RESPECT AND RESPONSIBILITY

*Don't ask yourself what the world needs. Ask yourself what makes you
come alive, and go do that, because what the world needs is people who
have come alive.* — Howard Thurman

There are many ways to catalyze our energies toward social change. The
bumps in the road lie not in finding sources of inspiration or provocation, but
in finding forms of action that bring us most alive and that we can sustain in
the face of all the ways we will be tested to stay the course. What the world
needs is for us to be awake and enlivened. Love will take us the rest of the way.

Taking action on behalf of the larger world reveals our essential belonging and acknowledges our interconnection. Acting for the common good also
works to establish our autonomy and lift up our unique contributions and
values. To act is to accept the proposition that we each matter and make a difference, no matter what we are told to the contrary. Life is messy and our decisions often imperfect, but in times like these, perfect is the enemy of the good.

The starfish parable, created by anthropologist Loren Eiseley, reminds
us that individual gestures do matter: *An old man is walking on a beach one*

day when he sees a boy repeatedly picking things up from the sand and tossing them into the ocean. The man approaches and asks the boy what he is doing. The boy replies that he is throwing starfish into the sea so they will not die in the sun. Looking at all the starfish and the miles of beach stretched out ahead of them, the old man suggests that, despite all his effort, the boy could not make much of a difference. The boy listens politely, bends down to pick up another starfish, and tosses it into the sea, saying, "I made a difference to that one." The next morning the old man could be seen alongside the boy tossing starfish into the water.

Our unequivocal gratitude for the preciousness of the world makes us want to protect it, one starfish, tree, person, community, initiative, or day at a time. Gratitude awakens respect and responsibility. We feel our interconnectedness, and the pain and beauty of belonging. Being grateful in difficult times, we can feel the suffering of others, make use of our blessings, and be compelled to act from a place that is engaged, self-responsible, and resourced. Grateful living helps by steadying us and bringing perspective, while also freeing and moving us to act in such a way that can help to bend history, even ever so slightly, in the direction of love.

These may be tough times to feel grateful. But denying all that is worthy of our gratitude does not protect us — nor does it help anyone or anything. Living gratefully is not about being Pollyannaish or putting our head in the sand. Gratefulness faces squarely that wonder and suffering live side by side, as do disaster and beauty. Grateful living helps us to never forget that we make the biggest difference through remaining connected to what we treasure, what we want to protect, and what truly matters most.

✳

When you feel grateful for someone or something, how does
that inspire a feeling of respect? What kinds of actions
does this inspire?

✳

How does a sense of responsibility support your ability
to be responsive?

AWAKEN THE POSSIBLITY OF HEALING

In a time of destruction, create something: a poem, a parade, a
community, a school, a vow, a moral principle; one peaceful moment.
— Maxine Hong Kingston

The needs of the world are a cry we cannot afford to ignore. The needs of our relationships and communities call for more compassion and engagement. The needs of our own hearts compel us to crack open and connect. Making a meaningful difference requires values-aligned, heart-aligned action. This is why grateful living is so promising — it offers an accessible path to transform our relationship to life, and in so doing to contribute to transforming life for others. Grateful living asks us to *stop* and experience our heart's truth, to *look* in order to notice the opportunities we have at hand to make a difference, and to *go* by taking action that can help foster a peaceful, loving world that is sacred for all.

Tapping into our hearts and listening deeply, we may be called to do something we have never done before. Now is the time to muster our creativity and courage. Doing something — anything — that expresses our gratitude and clarity of heart is very moving; it will move those around us, and perhaps the dial of the world.

When activism unites us with our heartfelt values and joys, we find ease and pleasure in the doing, making it more likely we can stay the course. Love to make art? Paint posters and postcards. Love to write? Blogs and poems are forms of activism, too. Love to be quiet? Sit vigil. Love to connect with people? Organize with like-minded others. Movements for change succeed and thrive when many different kinds of people can find ways to express themselves. We are always in need of new forms of creative activism as the conditions around us transform. The important thing is for each of us to do something meaningful to take a stand when our values and hearts are ignited.

What if we allowed the vastness of love to point and lead the way? What if we let gratitude be an activating experience that leads us to joyful, passionate action? What if we tune in to our fierce hearts with regard for ourselves and each other, our ancestors, and future generations? Let us raise our individual and collective voices in a hopeful, loving chorus that drowns out efforts to silence or erase any of us.

✳

How could living and acting from gratitude make a healing difference
in your community? What might that look like?

✳

When you act based on what you are grateful for, how are your
actions likely to be different than when you act from anger or
obligation? How might your actions be experienced differently?

BENEDICTION

May you taste the colors of sunset,
may you touch the chorus of dawn,
may your eyes turn toward the beauty
even when it's gone.
May you weave a path of blessing
through ecstasy and grief.
May you tend the flame within you
may you feed it with belief.
May you find yourself in strangers
and meet them within you.
May you trust that we are windows
the world is peering through.
May you linger in each moment,
receiving with your heart
the gift of possibilities
that presence can impart.
May you become a portal
to the love behind your toil,
may you become a silence
within the world's turmoil.
May the prayers that grow within you
bloom in many lands.
We are woven of connections
and peace is in our hands.
— Bernadette Miller

GRATEFUL FOR EACH MOMENT

The true meaning of life is to plant trees under whose shade you do not expect to sit. — Nelson Henderson

There is a wake-up call happening in our world. Forces are at work that threaten our social covenants, civil rights, and diverse communities — indeed, the safety of our planet and global family. Forces for social change, justice, love, and peace are also at work. If we value living in a democracy, then we have to stay awake and remain at work for it. Participation matters. Showing up for our beliefs matters. Taking a stand matters.

Grateful living invites us to connect with the things that matter most, and to recognize these commitments as an integral part of our ongoing effort to make life better for all. It stimulates our inherent passion to preserve and protect what we value, and therefore to empathize and align with the needs and values of others. It reminds us of all that we have going for us, and all the ways that we can leverage our good fortune. Grateful living helps us to sustain our actions on behalf of the natural world and human community by continually reminding and supporting us to recognize that we are part of something far larger than ourselves. It offers the nourishment of a consistent wellspring of principles and practices that can truly guide and sustain us in the sacred work, and the very long haul, of loving this world.

✳

May you hold the needs of the world with respect and responsibility.

Practices and Prompts

STOP. LOOK. GO. PRACTICE

Grateful Activism

Even superheroes chart their course. Take a moment to pause and reflect before moving forward with intention. By connecting to our breath and gratitude first, we are better able to find our focus and become more strategic in our actions.

When we look outside ourselves, we recognize that we are not alone; we are one among many who are part of a long history of activism and change. We can gain inspiration from remembering that through ongoing, collective action people have made a difference. With an expanded gaze we are able to learn from those who came before us and those who surround us, and we can find the hope we need, in ourselves and each other, to do what we feel called to do.

> **Stop:** Slow down and become cognizant of the intense privileges and blessings of being awake and alive. Claiming the gifts of our lives is not an indulgence. Instead, we are reminded of what we have going for us that many in the world do not. Stopping helps us connect with the deepest truths and concerns of our hearts, to become grounded in our bodies and in our awareness. This perspective allows us to shine more brightly with a sense of possibility and responsibility to improve life for others, in the ways that we can.

> **Look:** Notice your surroundings and the resources and passions with which you can make a difference. Looking within helps you to connect to your sense of purpose and your fundamental principles, rather than feeling scattered and reactive. Firmly believing in the sacredness of your values, and being clear about what you love and cherish, you can stand your ground with integrity and resolve, and be enlivened in the process.

Go: When you actively take a stand for the things for which you are most grateful, your actions are sourced differently. Committed to what you treasure most deeply, you can uncover reserves of vigor and clarity to fuel and sustain your activism. Actions that arise from grateful awareness are creative, relevant, effective, sustaining, and meaningful. Find the issues that ignite your heart's concern, the paths of expression that are most meaningful for you, and go forth.

- Grateful for democracy? Uphold it.
- Grateful for diversity? Protect it.
- Grateful for our Earth? Care for it.
- Grateful for freedom? Defend it.
- Grateful for love? Spread it.
- Grateful for justice? Fortify it.
- Grateful for peace? Live it.

Draw on Your Wellspring

Sit quietly to connect with love and the fullness of your heart as an endless well to nourish and bless your concerns for the world. Visualize this wellspring as an inexhaustible source inside you. Just as you would heed love to direct you to tend the hurts of a child, you can heed love to direct you to tend needs on a larger scale. Ask yourself: How is love moving me to tend the hurts in the world? How are the things I am grateful for offering me guidance? Where are the opportunities available for me to offer love? Let yourself know that, connected to your heart, you will be filled up the more that you pour yourself out.

Take a Grateful Stand

What are your core values? You can use the Five Guiding Principles if you'd like — the point is to know what moves and motivates your actions so you can be guided by what matters most to you. Write down your guiding values or principles and keep them where you can be reminded of them throughout your day. When you act in alignment with these, you are standing for your deep convictions. When something is out of alignment, you will be supported to take a stand.

How would you like these commitments to show up more powerfully as you think of bringing yourself to address the hurts around you and in the larger world? Lean into them for guidance as you seek to live in greater alignment while having greater impact.

PERSPECTIVE PROMPTS
Let Discernment Guide You

There is a place of balance between feeling that we have all the time in the world and no time at all, between feeling overwhelmed to the point of hysteria and overwhelmed to a state of lethargy. None of these extremes activate us toward sustainable engagement. When we are awakened to poignancy rather than panic — knowing that life is meaningful and that time may be finite but still offers spaciousness within which we can act — we are able to come alive to this moment, this human family, this planet.

Allow yourself to feel the fleetingness of time and the preciousness of all that you love to the precise degree that it moves and activates you to offer your creative, compassionate gifts.

✳

I follow the cries and joys of my heart to meet those of the world.

You Are Part of Something Larger

As we feel ourselves more interconnected, we discover a responsibility for being one with the natural world and human family. Doubting this preserves the status quo. Believing that we each have the capacity for impact has motivated millions of individuals to do what they could throughout history. Thoughtful, committed citizens have long made it their business to change the world for the better. Surprising acts have changed the course of history: the stand-offs in Tiananmen Square, the opposition to apartheid in South Africa, the pipeline protests at Standing Rock, the nonviolent resistance of the American civil rights movement. The collective includes each of us.

Consider yourself one among many thoughtful, committed citizens, who — in small ways, over time — have shifted the dial. Surprise yourself with your vision and courage.

✳

When I am moved to act, I am part of a long-time, vast movement for change.

Use Your Blessings

It is only when we claim the blessings we have that we can make use of them to have an impact — not from a place of guilt but from responsibility. Our ordinary is truly someone else's extraordinary. If we have money (even a little) and we are thankful, we can put it to use and share it. If we have a body that works, we can count ourselves fortunate, help get things done, help others, and offer care. If we have education, strengths, or skills, they are gifts longing to be uplifted and of use.

Think about how resources that are sufficient in your life could be of use to the larger world. Only when we recognize and fully acknowledge our plenty can we make a difference with what we have.

✳

My good fortune can be of service in meeting the unmet needs of others.

Take a Stand for What Matters

Times of societal upheaval call on us to know what we stand for and compel us to act with courage on behalf of those values. When our core values are in discord with what we see around us, it is vital to deepen our commitment to our principles, to make sure that they are explicit and unequivocal in our hearts, articulated in our lives, and expressed with clarity when called for. Knowing what we stand for helps us to know very clearly what we will not stand for, and vice versa. Tending to the principles we appreciate most is empowering and enlightening.

Live like a tuning fork, able to sense whether what is happening around you is in or out of harmony with what you value. Take a stand when your core principles are compromised.

✳

I can lean into the heart of my core values for clarity and conviction.

Let Love Sing

Being of service can be a source of profound joy. Love is a verb — it wants to be active. It wants to heal. It wants to be witnessed, felt, demonstrated, shared, and flung and sung from treetops. Love does not want to be subordinated to grief and hurt; it wants to be part of it. Love is longing to be woven into the entire emotional fabric of our lives. Love wants the opportunity to make a difference, and when we offer love to others, it changes the landscape of our reality. Love is a transformative power.

Extend yourself creatively and joyfully with a thoughtful gesture of love to someone who is in need, and notice the shifts that take place within you, and around you. Extend yourself to communities in need to make an even bigger difference.

✳

Love is a verb. Serve is a verb. Enjoy is a verb. I love making
verbs active in my life.

CHAPTER 13

LIVING A GRATEFUL LEGACY

Onward Ho!

Looking back, I realize that perspective was among the greatest gifts I earned in facing cancer. I earned it through a rigorous curriculum that taught me to be unceasingly present to everything life brought my way. I also earned perspective by practicing radical hospitality for: Generosity that took my breath away. Pain that left me breathless. Vulnerability that laid me bare. Love that kept me afloat. News that sank me. Hope that lifted my spirits. Losses that flattened me. Fear that tenderized my heart. Mortality that woke me up. Encouragement and discouragement that eventually simply became courage.

Grateful perspectives do not protect us from the challenges of life, but they do offer us the means to navigate them. As of this writing, I am 26 years posttreatment. I truly never expected to live this long. Honestly, each year I am here strikes me as nothing short of a mind-blowing miracle and privilege.

People who survive cancer treatments as aggressive as mine, and who live for as long as I have, can expect a host of long-term acute and chronic effects, as well as high risk for secondary cancers. This is part of the unspoken survivor's contract. I have been host to my share of these, and they are likely to keep coming. Managing chronic vertigo from an intractable spinal cerebrospinal fluid leak where I had my surgery and radiation has made life challenging to navigate with ease or equanimity. Sometimes it is manageable, sometimes quite disabling. Regardless, surviving is a teacher — keeping me compassionate and humbled, reminding me that I am lucky to be alive and that having a body may have its burdens but it is a blessing nonetheless. I am always reminded that in the fact of being here at all, I am one of the lucky ones. There is no forgetting these things.

Cancer took me to the edge of existence as I knew it and let me peer into possibilities I had not faced before. I stayed looking a long while at the darkness that lurked there and was not sure I would emerge. I learned that our humanness breaks us as it makes us, and our hurts connect us with one another and to life when we meet each other in these liminal places we often avoid. Among these places is the mystery of joy and how it lives side by side with struggle. Walking — or at times being carried — along the cliff's edge of uncertainty helped me learn to be with suffering, my own and that of others. It made me better able to recognize the kin of my heart. And it helped me learn about what truly matters. What is ephemeral. What remains.

I choose to honor the teachings of my cancer journey by keeping them close because all the lessons I learned during and immediately after cancer continue to have relevance. I have the gifts and challenges of a survivor's life, of any human life. But I find that pretty much everything falls into a context of great privilege when I remind myself that it could have been otherwise. When I am loyal to what I have learned, I experience all my moments as unexpected gifts. I am able to see the ordinary as extraordinary and take very little for granted. I am constantly surprised by myself and how life unfolds itself in my days. And within this, I see that my experiences are very much shaped by where I direct my attention, and so I am reminded to appreciate and tend the people and things I value. And love — well, love is the essential joy that life allows. My legacy will hopefully be that of a heart that lived out loud and rarely ran for cover.

What can bring us back from the precarious edges of uncertainty and suffering to live life fully in the day-to-day beauty and difficulties of the here and now? The answer is in not wanting or waiting for some moment other than the one that is here, but instead seeing and seizing this moment — and all its opportunity — as ours for the living.

I am surely no more courageous in the face of challenges or capable of grateful living than anyone else. As a matter of fact, much less so than many people who inspire me. I never knew I could face what I faced until I faced it. None of us do. Any perspective I developed that helps me to live gratefully has been both handed to me by chance and hard-won. I am the first to admit that I still lose perspective over and over again. I am simply dogged in remembering the gifts that a grateful perspective has offered my life and I am commited to find my way back to it again and again. I am ever drawn to the light of what rings as truth and liberates the heart.

My deepest wish is that we might all learn to more fully trust and appreciate the opportunities, moments, people, and gifts of our lives without needing to lose, or nearly lose them, to know — and show — that they matter. If wake-up calls can come into lives that are already awake to how much we have to be grateful for, then we will not need them. We will already be living fully aware of what matters to us, alert to joy and beauty, and attentive to love. May it be so. May grateful living help show us the way.

THE WHOLEHEARTED JOURNEY OF OUR LIVES

The antidote to exhaustion is wholeheartedness.
— Brother David Steindl-Rast

In the end, we all want to have lived lives that mattered. We all want to have left a lasting imprint on the hearts of those we loved and on the world as a whole. We all want to be remembered for the best of who we are and how we lived. Opportunities abound to fulfill these deeply human longings. But we often miss making the connection that *now* is the portal to *then*. We miss seeing that the choices we make at every juncture of our current moments are decisions that either lead us toward or away from the possibility that we will be held as we want to be held in the end. Waking up and living fully today is the only way to be remembered in the ways that matter to us when that great unknowable culmination of life finally arrives.

Grateful living offers us a way to approach life with resilience and joy in the face of its mysteries, difficulties, and even its loss. It directs us toward what matters, what is meaningful, and what will make a difference in the hearts of those with whom we are navigating this lifetime. It weds us to living every moment and every thing as if it matters, because it does.

BECOME PRESENT TO THE LEGACY OF YOUR LIFE

If I am not for myself, who will be for me? And when I am for myself, what am I? And if not now, when? — Hillel the Elder

The moment we bring awareness to the basic idea that we will have a legacy, we begin to create one that matters. With our choices. With our attention. With our moments. Acknowledgment of legacy itself brings home the realization that we will not live forever and that we are shaping and living our legacy now. Awareness of our impermanence enhances our ability to occupy and tend the moments we have. Embracing it supports us to hold a space for greater presence and aliveness in our lives.

Presence is simply the price of admission for a meaningful life — this is why we *pay* attention. We cannot afford to be anywhere else but here. The time we spend anticipating the future or lamenting the past is lost to us. Finding ways to repeatedly come back to presence will open the doors and windows to opportunity when it knocks. And opportunity is knocking all the time.

It may be challenging to be truly present to all of life, but it is imperative for those of us who want how we live to be a reflection of what is most important to us. We need to live on purpose. Living with intention will serve the creation of the life we most want to live and leave behind. Present moment attention and intention is how we negotiate a life of more alignment and fewer regrets. So what might you be waiting for? Whose permission do you think you need in order to live your most great, full life? Your most grateful life? What is it that your heart wants to do with the opportunities of this life you have been given?

✳

How does the notion of legacy move or motivate you?

✳

Does imagining that you are living your legacy now shift your relationship to being present? If so, how?

VOICES OF GRATEFUL LIVING

There is no more important work for the soul than to cultivate the path of living gratefully. All else will be managed in a robust and generous way. Everything thrives through the awareness of the great fullness of life as gift. — Chuck R.

SEEK A PERPSECTIVE OF WHOLEHEARTED TRUST IN LIFE

We can only be said to be alive in those moments when our hearts are conscious of our treasures. — Thornton Wilder

Whenever we embrace the vulnerability that comes with being alive and which inherently accompanies living gratefully, we are reminded that time is limited, so we should treasure and trust the life we have now. Holding this poignant perspective is how legacy is created — not missing an opportunity while opportunities are available to us.

Trust in life is a lesson that many of us may wrestle with in a variety of ways, but also one that delivers unparalleled opportunities. What does this mean for each of us? Surely the idea of trusting life lands differently into each of our lives, and at different stages. Trusting life is a powerful practice; it is a way of receiving life that allows us to harvest meaning and learning from whatever surfaces. Like mindfulness or grateful living practice, it is not when every moment of our commitment unfolds "perfectly" that we consider ourselves to have an effective practice. Meaning is made in noticing one more moment of awareness, one more centimeter of possibility, one more instance of trust. Our "success" is earned in returning again and again to the invitation and opportunities that trusting life extends to us.

Ultimately, perspective helps us to recognize that each moment and each interaction, every step on the path and every direction we turn, can be infused with a sense of all that is poignant and precious. This is how meaningful legacies are made — one grateful, wholehearted moment and choice at a time.

❋

How can you invite greater trust into your life? How do you experience its presence?

❋

What does it mean to you to live wholeheartedly? How might this be connected to trust in life?

AWAKEN TO THE POSSIBILITY OF LIVING YOUR LEGACY

Why not move into your house of joy and shine into every crevice!
For you are the secret Treasure-bearer,
and always have been.
Didn't you know? — Rumi

There are teachers all around us telling us not to sleepwalk our lives away. There are poems, stories, experiences, and people everywhere reminding us how much these moments that we are alive mean and matter. If we tune in to the sky, the Earth, the human heart, we can hear the world imploring us in every way to remember: *Be grateful for this moment; this moment is your life.*

What could be more important than cultivating a sense of more grateful presence, perspective, and possibility as we move through our days? What better way could there be to honor this life we have been given than with gratefulness and great fullness of heart in its heart-wrenching, heart-awakening aliveness. This is no less than life deserves from us. This is no less than we deserve from life.

Possibility beckons. It sits everywhere in wait for our discovery and our creation. Possibility is what the future is made from. This moment — with wholehearted engagement — allows us to shape the lives we want to leave behind. Living gratefully is one of the most powerful ways we reduce our regrets. Live in the ways that you want to be remembered. Live in the ways that you know in your heart matter and will be enduring. Live in ways that serve love. Live such that your life opens doors and hearts for others. Plant trees that others will sit beneath. Sow seeds now that will nourish future generations.

Will you make your life a living embodiment of — and testament to — the possibilities that gratefulness awakens in you? Let your life right now be your answer.

✳

What can you do today to nurture one new possibility for the life and legacy you are living now?

✳

What could you do to nurture one new possibility for life after you are no longer here — your future legacy?

VOICES OF GRATEFUL LIVING

By making time to be still, my true nature has an opportunity to be felt. A snow globe, after shaken and left to be still, begins the process of settling down and clarifying the water within. By intentionally parking my brain in front of gratefulness, it allows it to collect evidence for the marvelous, beautiful, deep world we move through. Then, my heart not only beats but radiates within my body, its energy extending out to others.

— Kat K.

Hokusai Says

Hokusai says look carefully.
He says pay attention, notice.
He says keep looking, stay curious.
He says there is no end to seeing.
He says look forward to getting old.
He says keep changing,
you just get more who you really are.
He says get stuck, accept it, repeat
yourself as long as it is interesting.
He says keep doing what you love.

He says keep praying.

He says every one of us is a child,
every one of us is ancient,
every one of us has a body.
He says every one of us is frightened.
He says every one of us has to find
a way to live with fear.
He says everything is alive —
shells, buildings, people, fish,
mountains, trees, wood is alive.
Water is alive.

Everything has its own life.
Everything lives inside us.
He says live with the world inside you.
He says it doesn't matter if you draw,
or write books. It doesn't matter
if you saw wood, or catch fish.
It doesn't matter if you sit at home
and stare at the ants on your veranda
or the shadows of the trees
and grasses in your garden.
It matters that you care.

It matters that you feel.
It matters that you notice.
It matters that life lives through you.
Contentment is life living through you.
Joy is life living through you.
Satisfaction and strength
is life living through you.
He says don't be afraid.
Don't be afraid.
Love, feel, let life take you by the hand.
Let life live through you.
— Roger S. Keyes

GRATEFUL FOR EACH MOMENT

Tomorrow belongs to those of us who conceive of it as belonging to
everyone; who lend the best of ourselves to it, and with joy. — Audre Lorde

Joy is the gift of aliveness coming to life. Enjoyment is our birthright and it
can be a part of our legacy in as many moments as we can discover it. Joy
is often harvested directly out of our difficulties, from the ashes of experiences that — once metabolized — offer us perspective about what matters.
Wholeheartedness can be as simple as connecting with certainty about what
is meaningful to you in a given moment and letting that certainty shine forth
from you and from the entirety of your life. The wholehearted choices you
make in your moments today can be the birthplace for joy now, and the birthplace of your legacy when the time comes.

"Grateful living is just another way of speaking about full aliveness. It is
to wake up to the joy of life," says Brother David. We are well-served to follow
the path of wholehearted aliveness for the opportunities offered to us in this
mysterious, marvelous, messy experience of being alive.

✳

May you hold every moment as an opportunity to live
wholeheartedly, with trust in life.

Practices and Prompts

STOP. LOOK. GO. PRACTICE
Grateful Remembrance

Get a pen and paper and make sure you are in a quiet, comfortable place where you can spend some time with this visualization and reflection.

Stop: Imagine a gathering that will be held after your life is over, with your favorite people in attendance. Invite yourself to befriend this idea and the images that it will evoke. This occasion is a testament to your life. It is a celebration, and each person in attendance will cite the top three things that they appreciate about you, what you taught them, or what you brought to their life. Take a few breaths and allow yourself to bring this future possibility into your mind's eye. Gently notice and acknowledge the feelings this brings up.

Look: Take a few minutes to bring detail to this image. Where is this special gathering being held? Imagine a special convening place. What is the energy of the gathering? Is it reverent? Joyful? Festive? Solemn? Sacred? Is it all of that and more? Imagine the energy in the space. Who are the people you hope will speak up? Imagine them each present for the occasion and taking a few minutes to speak.

What are some of the memories, stories, qualities, actions, and offerings that you hope will be cited about you? Imagine these things being shared. How would you like to be remembered? Paint a picture in your mind of how you want to be thought about when you are no longer here. Write these reflections down on paper.

Go: Make a word collage or a list of the words that stand out in your future reflection. Make it creative or make it practical. Use this list to guide you in making choices about how to focus your energy and attention today and every day. If you do this more and more, following guidance about how you want your legacy to live on after you, you will live your legacy now. It is both an honor and a privilege to serve your life in this way. Treat it gratefully.

Trust in Life

Look back to the times when you have placed your trust in life, when you have surrendered yourself to the flow of the river and let it carry you. It is very important that we build ourselves a reliable index of memories of how life has made itself known to us as trustworthy, even if our minds quarrel with the concept. The mind may gravitate to stock-piling memories of times when our fears were proven true or when life disappointed or hurt us, but the number of moments when life did not fail us far exceed those. Every time we come through something diffi-cult a little wiser, follow our intuition, let ourselves be surprised by life's unfolding instead of controlling it, we give life a second chance. You have a 100 percent survival rate to date. This is all worthy reinforce-ment for putting your trust in life.

PERSPECTIVE PROMPTS
Embrace the Paradox of Poignancy

Poignancy — holding the awareness of what is meaningful in the same space as we hold the awareness of limited time — is the defining characteristic of legacy. We will be hard-pressed to consider anything as traditional as legacy planning, living wills, estate plans, or end-of-life issues without racing head-long into poignant feelings. In the midst of our normal days, poignancy is a paradox, reminding us that life is defined by limited time. When we are con-sidering the limited nature of our existence here, poignancy helps us to focus on the fact that we are still very much alive.

Notice the kinds of paradoxical feelings that consideration of your legacy opens up for you. Feel welcomed by the tremendous number of opportunities you have today to shape your life.

※

I am grateful to be alive with countless moments available to me.

The Reverberations of Legacy

If legacy is the culmination of our choices, everyone who has ever lived has left a legacy of some kind. People such as Anne Frank leave a legacy with significant reverberations even though they only lived short lives. It does not take a long life to leave a substantive legacy, but it takes intention. We could also say that many of the people who left legacies that have impacted us and the world the most are those who were able to find ways to be grateful for the gifts and opportunities available to them, taking a stand for what mattered most to them, even in the most trying or short-lived circumstances.

Think of some of the people whose legacies have inspired you the most and consider their common characteristics. Become more aware of the inspiration available to you.

I am blessed to be able to live and shape my legacy now.

The Privilege of Being Alive

The ability to even consider our legacies rests solely on the fact that we are here and breathing, fully alive. Many people who wanted to be alive today and to have the chance to think about their options are no longer here for the blessing of this consideration. No matter how old we are and no matter the condition of our bodies, minds, or spirits, our very aliveness is a fact to be celebrated, not taken for granted.

Consider the privilege afforded to you by the fact of your being alive. Think of the choices you want to make with the moments and opportunities you have right now, and with those that are ahead of you.

It is a privilege to be alive in all of my moments, no matter what.

Your Choices Shape Your Legacy

Our legacies are made from the choices we make, and at their best they will reflect our deep beliefs and core values. Grateful living principles help to guide our lives and legacy to embody what we hold most dear. We are continually oriented and reoriented toward ways of being that fortify the heart: generosity, compassion, reverence, respect, humility, joy, and more. These are the kinds of words we will want etched on our tombstones and in the hearts of those who will remember us after we have gone.

Imagine yourself remembered for the qualities that you hold most dear and make choices today that will help you to be who you want to be memorialized for being.

❋

I am embodying the aspects of myself that I want to have remembered.

The Ultimate Legacy Is Love

Joyful memory is the terrain of joyful legacy. It is what will sustain us in profound ways as we make meaning of our lives in our final years, and it will sustain our loved ones once we are gone. There is no legacy greater than love. And there is also no opportunity to bring forth pleasure greater than how we show our love. No matter what, the love and care we leave in the hearts of others will be what we are remembered for. Love has staying power. Love is transformative. Our love for life will be the indelible signature we leave behind, and with it will be all of the hearts we have signed with our affection.

Consider where the threads of joyful connection are strong in your life, and where they could be strengthened. Let investing in love today be your grateful living legacy.

❋

My greatest legacy is love. I make it matter every day.

> *What you seek is seeking you.*
> —Rumi

EPILOGUE

When I completed cancer treatments in 1993, I could not write. Anything. At all. For a long time. Chemotherapy had caused peripheral neuropathy, which kept me from being able to type or hold a pen with ease; and I suffered the residual blur of chemo brain. But none of that is what actually kept me from writing.

I could not write because I did not want to spend a single moment unavailable to my life as it was unfolding. I had been awakened to see each day as a blessing and my heart had been opened to the brevity of time. I did not want to squander any of my life with an absence of attention to my immediate experiences, loved ones, and the beauty around me. Even though many people encouraged me to pick up my old writing practice, or to document my survivor's story for the benefit of others, I simply could not bring myself to sit and try to capture anything in words. Life itself wanted to keep me busy, calling me loudly at all hours to behold a canopy of stars, chase sunlight, tend to my body and heart, or revel in the proximity of love in its many forms. For years, writing felt like it stole me from life, pulling me out of *experiencing* my moments in lieu of thinking and theorizing about them. And in many ways it still does.

When I wake up to each new day now, I am surely grateful. And, to be honest, urgency and intensity are awakened in me as well. I wonder how to act on the fact that life is so beautiful and also finite. What do I do with the gift of the moment? How do I invest in even the *near future* knowing that the future itself is unpromised? Aware that my life is precious, how do I make sense of spending countless hours each day sitting at a computer? It can be a recurring conundrum for me, and reconciling my choices is often a wildly inelegant dance. But being fully awake to conundrums is the price of admission to a conscious life. And it is worth everything it takes for me to fumble my way through figuring it out — because this is my perfectly imperfect practice of grateful living.

From the beginning, writing this book felt more like a "soul assignment" than a decision. This was fortunate, as I would have sidelined myself a million times for anything less than a burning mandate from the universe. These words mark the endpoint of an effort that took more resolve than I imagined I was capable of mustering. Like a pilgrimage, the book took me on an arduous journey away from the pull of my day-to-day life and asked me to focus intently on a commitment to completion — no matter what. I can now attest to the fact that in the midst of it, something profound in me changed. Holding fast to gratefulness, my trust in life was tested and deepened. I came to reconcile the needs of this moment with those of a tomorrow worth investing and believing in. For someone who has lived acutely for a long time — dancing with life on the head of a pin, so to speak — this journey turned out to be more trying, and also more healing than I imagined.

While working on this book, my mother was unexpectedly given a terminal diagnosis and died. I spent much of the six months she was in hospice digging my heels in, resisting the possibility that I could actually midwife the birth of a first book and help to midwife the end of my mother's life simultaneously. Ultimately, it was this nexus of birth and death that humbled me, calling me to embrace, face squarely, and reconcile anything I would have to say about living gratefully with the full-blown reality of life. Whatever I was going to write would need to stand up to an active engagement with the great fullness of life, and an active connection to what matters most — in the very midst of losing what matters most.

It was through offering myself fully to all of what life asked of me this last year — loss, grieving, writing, and surviving — that grateful living evolved from an "idea" to a true way of life. In the process of the book's unfolding, what seemed true was tested and either became *more* true or was discarded. What I had always told people was nourishing about gratefulness ended up nourishing me to my core and carrying me through. As words poured and petered out of me, it was as though each one had to go through the fact-check and filter of an exhausted, broken heart. The process — and what survived the process — became my medicine.

As I sit writing these words today, the medicinal power of gratefulness is needed in our world more than I could have imagined only weeks ago. It is early 2020, a time that will be forever known as the awakening of the COVID-19 pandemic. Each day another city, state, or community in North America is turning to "shelter in place." Together, we are trying to flatten the curve and contain the spread. We are confronted as a nation and a globe with unparalleled uncertainty. We are reminded anew of what is actually essential. We are questioning and ceasing many aspects of our daily lives, enduring days of greater isolation, fear in the face of the unknown, and suffering with what *is* known. Try as we might, we have absolutely no idea what will unfold from here, but we do know that we will be challenged. And we also know that we will be presented with abundant opportunities to reorient ourselves toward a way of life that is sustainable and recognizes our interdependence; one that exhibits greater appreciation for one another and all of Life. And like any pilgrimage worth the journey, we will learn a lot about ourselves and about love — if we commit to taking nothing in our lives for granted, and continually say *yes* to the invitations for transformation we are extended.

Grateful living makes life your pilgrimage and all your moments a practice ground. It offers a path rich with reminders that point you again and again toward the place where your heart can remember and come alive to what matters most. It invites you to return to this remembrance and heightened aliveness, no matter how far afield you — or the world — may feel. Each time you stop on the path for presence, look for perspective, and go toward possibility, you will recognize and appreciate the opportunities available to you, no matter your circumstances.

There are times when the path of life will turn a corner and deliver you the blessing of perspective. Whenever and however perspective arrives, know you are being offered a gift and say *yes*. This is what waking up is about, and it will change how you want to live. Time will feel more vivid, more precious, more transient. This awareness can be a welcome shift. Poignancy is likely to grab hold of you and reorder your priorities. Let it have its way with you. An experience of privilege will fill you up. Let yourself be moved. Peak awareness will offer you a sense of belonging. Let yourself connect. Your principles will want to direct you to what matters. Let yourself be guided. The lure of beauty and pleasure will call to you more loudly. Let yourself go.

Life *is* a gift. Everything *is* surprise. The ordinary *is* extraordinary. Appreciation *is* generative. Love *is* transformative. These truths are seeking you in every moment. Take nothing for granted. Wake up grateful. It is never too late. It is never too early. Say *yes* to your life.

BEYOND GRATEFUL

There have been more finish lines to cross in my lifetime than I care to count, and I have crossed most of them in the arms of loved ones. After almost two years of working on this book, I now see the delusion of my original hope to be a relaxed, low-maintenance, self-sufficient writer. The truth kept a small village of people very busy pulling, prodding, praying, and "patching me up" across this finish line. And I am truly beyond grateful. They all deserve a major shout-out. I wish I could put their names up in lights somewhere, but I hope and trust my thanks here will do.

For having guided me to be a person who could have even imagined writing a book about gratefulness, I have countless people to thank. I bow here to three beloved teachers: Jon Kabat-Zinn, with whom I first studied at Omega Institute in 1993. Meeting you and mindfulness meditation was love at first breath. You woke up my heart — and still do. Lynne Twist, who beckoned me cross-country in 2003 to help inspire a world committed to sufficiency. You taught me by example that generosity makes us rich — and still do. Br. David Steindl-Rast, whose way of being and teachings converged to be the work I knew could hold everything that mattered most to me. You showed me the path to aliveness — and still do.

For generously supporting and believing in this project before it had come fully into form, I want to thank The Fetzer Institute, Gay Hapgood, Missy Carter, and Susan and John. Your investment offered me the rare, invaluable opportunity for greater ease and exploration as *Wake Up Grateful* awakened.

For holding me throughout the writing process with professionalism, dedication, and stunning patience, I extend my heartfelt gratitude to writing coaches/editors Lisa Bennett, Sage Cohen, and Rose Zonetti. I learned so much from each of you about "going above and beyond." And go beyond you did.

For sharing your beautiful, quiet homes so that I could write and edit, rewrite and re-edit more times than I care to mention, I offer thanks to the Thayer Family, Lorraine Sahagian and Ted Giles, Paula and Will Bundy, and Mark McDonough. You showed me the sacred generosity of sharing space as a form of love.

For nourishing me, I thank Alice Cozzolino for her "food as love," Jessie Childs for her kindness, and Saralee Hofrichter for filling me up on Fridays when my tank was on empty. Also, Didi Firman for her wise support as the book prepares to go to print. You each helped me keep calm and carry on.

For trustworthy and treasured friendship during this difficult year, I am blessed with abundance. A special shout-out goes to my long-time BFF, Martha Davis, who offered weekly encouragement and smarts, as well as support whenever needed, which was always. Also, thanks to "the Cones" — you know who you are. To Tesa Silvestre, Laura Loescher, Tuti Scott, and Jaij Wood — your long-distance, long-time love was sustaining. To Jenny Ladd, for weekly river-walk inspiration. To Ruth Folchman, Paula Bundy, Susan Clopton, Ellen Landis and Lisa Thompson, Ted Giles and Lorraine Sahagian, Betsy Dinger and Karen Jodoin, Deb Burkhalter, and Mark McDonough, thank you for showing up with me and for me on so many levels on so many days and in so many ways. And to the enduring memory and inspiration of Terri Schatz, Mary Ann Baker, and Paula Murphy . . . I am forever grateful.

For being the sister of my dreams, I acknowledge Martha Nelson Patrick. I could not do life without you; thank you for making it so I don't have to. For my dad, John Nelson, and the joie de vivre I continually learn from your example, I am deeply thankful. To Johnstone Campbell and Rennie Nelson, with gratitude for your enduring love. For my brothers Johnny, Seth, and Paul, you are each a blessing. For William and Greg Hannum, who lived with me while writing this book, and my extended out-law crew, thanks for being a loving family to me. And for my mom, Sandy, I miss you more than words can say — thank you for teaching me such tenacious will to live. I wish you were here to share in the joy of this book's completion.

To the Storey Publishing team, with their big spirit of welcome, aligned values, and commitment to grateful living, I am indebted. Most especially, to friend and publisher Deborah Balmuth, for saying yes and then following up with heart. To Alethea Morrison, for bringing such creative talent and commitment to this work. And to my inspiring, introverted editor Liz Bevilacqua for being an unexpected blessing on this adventure. Your appreciation and tolerance of this thin-skinned extrovert's process warrants a grand prize.

For their vision, patience, and abiding support, I offer my great gratitude to members of the board of directors of A Network for Grateful Living: Adetola Abiade, Michael Barton, Rocco Capobianco, Sheryl Chard, Anne Hiaring Hocking, Mary Kostel, Steve Rio, Alberto Rizzo, Chuck Roppel, Pear Urushima, and last but not least, Brother David Steindl-Rast. Your collective belief in me and this project made it plausible and possible. I am truly honored to serve this mission with you.

For the indomitable Gratefulness Team, I am moved and inspired by you every day. Katie Rubinstein, Saoirse McClory, Jeseph Meyers, Serafina Restaino, and Rose Zonetti — you each offer truly extraordinary commitment, heart, and skills to make grateful living the blessing to the world that it is. You carry our work with grace, gusto, and grit (when necessary). There are few honors greater than working, and walking through life, alongside you.

And finally, for Linda Hannum, a gratitude category all your own. Anything I thought I knew about loving partnership has been redefined by your commitment. You have offered me the most unfettered, unconditional, unimaginable understanding and encouragement for many years, but this year especially. You have been the steady voice beckoning me from the finish line, cheering by my side, and whispering the perfect prompt in my ear when I faltered. Your arms were — thankfully — never far, and I needed them more than either of us could have ever known. I am blessed every day by the generous love, gentle wisdom, and deep laughter you bring to my life. I can honestly say that this book, my life, and the world are far better because of you. And yes, that is a lot of 3s! Sometimes one word of praise simply will not do. You are so much reason to be grateful.

EXPLORING AND LEARNING MORE

A NETWORK FOR GRATEFUL LIVING

A Network for Grateful Living is a global nonprofit organization based in the United States that serves a growing movement of people who want to live more gratefully. It is the home to all Wake Up Grateful programs. Through a rich diversity of offerings, we support people to see the wonder and opportunity in every moment and to act boldly with love, generosity, and respect toward one another, ourselves, and the Earth. Our commitment is for the gifts of grateful living to be available to people from all walks of life, and we strive to keep all that we do welcoming, inclusive, and accessible. As a community of practice, we believe in the exponential impact of grateful living, so we create opportunities for people to gather and learn together, both online and in person.

Our organization was founded in 2000 by Brother David Steindl-Rast, known as the "grandfather of gratitude" and one of the most important figures in the modern interfaith dialogue movement. Having Brother David at the heart of our genesis story and our offerings is a blessing.

Exploring and Learning More

A Network for Grateful Living offers practices, resources, and belonging for those seeking a more awake, joyful, and meaning-filled life. We provide opportunities for personal reflection and simple ways to bring the benefits of grateful living into your day-to-day life, through live online eCourses and practices, in-person events, and abundant offerings on our website. Be in touch at WakeUp@grateful.org. You can find all of the resources listed here as well as other offerings at www.grateful.org, where you can:

JOIN A COMMUNITY OF PRACTICE

- Join or start a Grateful Gathering in your area or online
- Attend Grateful Living and Wake Up Grateful Workshops or Events
- Participate in live or on-demand eCourses and extended Practices

NOURISH YOUR DAILY PRACTICE

Sign up to receive our daily Word for the Day, twice-monthly Grateful Offerings newsletter, or Poem a Month by email.

- Watch *A Grateful Day*, *Stop. Look. Go.*, and *Blessings*
- Explore our curated Poetry Collection
- Deepen your exploration in our Library of Resources
- Share your grateful sentiments with our free eCards
- Reflect on the Daily Question in the Practice Space online

International Partners

Find other content translations at grateful.org.

Netzwerk Dankbar Leben: German
http://www.dankbar-leben.org

Vivir Agradecidos: Spanish
https://www.viviragradecidos.org

Viver Agradecidos: Portuguese
http://www.viveragradecidos.org

REFLECTIVE QUESTIONS FOR YOUR PRACTICE

We see questions as a powerful practice in and of themselves, as they open us to greater perspective and possibility. Use questions such as these for daily journal prompts, conversation starters at gatherings, post them where you will regularly see them, or simply pause to consider them in your day.

What everyday happenings do I cherish?

What is one memory for which I am forever grateful?

What gives me hope? How can I nurture it?

What aspects of the natural world are a source of inspiration to me?

How is where I live a blessing?

How can I see and experience silence as a gift today?

Who are some of the people who have helped me, whom I have never met?

What one word could I focus on that could help me show up more gratefully?

What are some of the joys that come from being exactly the age I am right now?

What am I curious about?

How can I nurture a greater sense of harmony with life?

What discovery from my childhood continues to inform my life?

What new beginnings am I grateful for today?

What advice has made a big difference in my life?

When has collaborating with others made something better?

How can I make more space for beauty, for myself and others?

Who is a role model for contentment in my life? Why?

What are some of the deepest convictions I have yet to give voice to?

What can I do so that I end this day with reverence for it?

Without overthinking, what are 10 things I appreciate about myself?

Unafraid, what would my most outrageous expression of gratefulness be?

The Brother David Steindl-Rast Archives
Special Collections at the University of Massachusetts Amherst
http://scua.library.umass.edu/umarmot/steind-rast-david

Brother David's German Language Library
https://www.bibliothek-david-steindl-rast.ch/index.php

Aligned Organizations
We celebrate organizations that bring gratefulness to life. These nonprofits offer inspiring resources, programs, and models for individuals and communities to deepen gratefulness. Learn more and engage through their offerings.

Greater Good Science Center
https://greatergood.berkeley.edu
The Greater Good Science Center studies the psychology, sociology, and neuroscience of well-being, and teaches skills that foster a thriving, resilient, and compassionate society.

The Nature of Gratitude
https://natureofgratitude.com
The Nature of Gratitude is an ensemble of artists who explore and share their love of nature and gratitude using music, spoken word, and photography.

Spirituality & Practice
https://www.spiritualityandpractice.com/
Spirituality & Practice is a multifaith and interspiritual website offering resources for spiritual journeys. They envision a global community vitally engaged with the wisdom and practices of the spiritual traditions.

Pachamama Alliance
https://pachamama.org
Pachamama Alliance is a global community helping people learn, connect, engage, travel, and cherish life in order to create a sustainable future that works for all.

The On Being Project

https://onbeing.org

The On Being Project takes up the animating questions at the center of life. It pursues wisdom and moral imagination as much as knowledge; nuance and poetry as much as fact. They seed human change that makes social change possible.

ServiceSpace

https://www.servicespace.org

ServiceSpace is run by volunteers, leveraging technology to encourage people around the world toward small acts of service. Their aim is to ignite the fundamental generosity that brings about inner and outer transformation.

Soul of Money Institute

https://soulofmoney.org

Soul of Money Institute aims to create a context of sufficiency, integrity, and responsibility for individuals and organizations in their relationship with money.

Look for the Good Project

https://lookforthegood.mykajabi.com/k-6program

This scientifically backed school-wide Gratitude Campaign Program helps K-6 parents and teachers unite around kindness for two weeks, positively impacting the school climate all year.

The Work That Reconnects

https://workthatreconnects.org

The Work That Reconnects, based in the teachings of Joanna Macy, unfolds as a journey that helps us experience firsthand that we are larger, stronger, more creative, and more deeply interconnected than we knew.

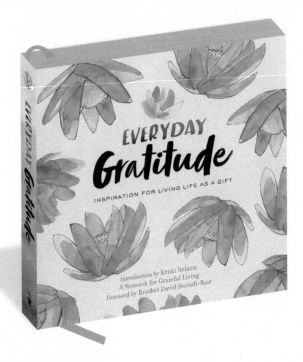

EVERYDAY GRATITUDE
Inspiration for Living Life as a Gift

by A Network for Grateful Living
Introduction by Kristi Nelson
Foreword by Brother David Steindl-Rast

Curated by A Network for Grateful Living, this beautiful collection offers inspiring quotes and thoughts from well-known minds such as Maya Angelou, Confucius, and Anne Frank combined with original reflections and practices to help you recognize the abundance of opportunities for gratitude and joy — all around you, every day. Hand-lettered art makes this a stunning gift to treasure, whether you keep it for yourself or give it to a loved one.